TOP **10**
VENICE

T0182359

CONTENTS

Introducing Venice

Top 10 Highlights

VENICE

INTRODUCING

Gondola on the Grand Canal

WELCOME TO
VENICE

Elegant, imaginative, iconic: that's Venice. Here, you can admire majestic Renaissance paintings, discover centuries-old crafts and travel by sleek gondola – all in one day. Don't want to miss a thing? With Top 10 Venice, you'll enjoy the very best the city has to offer.

With more UNESCO Heritage Sites than anywhere else in the world, Venice never fails to astonish. A cruise down the Grand Canal showcases a thousand years of architecture, from the Gothic Ca' d'Oro ("golden palace") to the glorious Baroque Santa Maria della Salute. More beautiful buildings can also be found in the Basilica of San Marco, a Byzantine gem seemingly created by angels, and the pretty-in-pink façade of Palazzo Ducale (Doge's Palace) which belies the prison cells within. Then, there's world-class art wherever you turn.

Architectural beauty of Venice

The Accademia museum is a storehouse of masterpieces, while the Peggy Guggenheim Collection is a modern-day showstopper, home to one of the most enviable stashes of modern art in the world. Embrace more of Venice's eclectic culture with a host of year-round festivals and events; there's no missing the famed Carnival, which sees Piazza San Marco overtaken by swarms of costumed, masked crowds. Gothic palaces, world-famous masterpieces and masquerade parties: this floating city floods the imagination with possibilities.

If you think that sounds thrilling, wait until you see what's hiding in the backstreets: glimpses of heaven in Tiepolo's frescoed palace ceilings, expert glass masters toiling at chandeliers that look like sea monsters, fishmongers hawking lagoon specialities at the Rialto market and chefs serving sensational *cicchetti* (Venetian tapas). In a city without wheels, every walk is a voyage of discovery. Experiencing the city by gondola is essential, but you'll also want to venture across the lagoon to see where Venice's story originated on the island of Torcello.

So, where to start? With Top 10 Venice, of course. This pocket-sized guide gets to the heart of the city with simple lists of 10, expert local knowledge and comprehensive maps, helping you turn an ordinary trip into an extraordinary one.

THE STORY OF
VENICE

Not content with conquering the known world with its navy, Venice dispatched explorers like Marco Polo to expand its trade horizons. When its empire declined, Venice refused to retreat from the world stage. Instead the city itself became a stage, attracting global audiences with vivid art, modern opera, independent thinkers and unparalleled parties.

Portrait engraving of Doge Orso Ipato, the first Venetian doge

Swamp to Empire

A malarial swamp is a strange place to build a city – unless you're under attack by Huns and Goths. So began the story of Venice in 452 CE, when Veneti refugees from Romanized cities (such as Aquileia on the mainland) first fled to the island of Torcello and then to surrounding islands. By 726 they had elected their first *dux* (Latin for leader; in Venetian "doge"), Orso Ipato, and by 811, the ducal capital had moved to a fortress on the Rivo Alto (Rialto), the shallowest part of the lagoon, inaccessible to most ships.

There, on the site of today's Piazza San Marco, they rose above their swampy circumstances by driving Alpine tree trunks into the silt and raising up palaces on impermeable platforms of Istrian stone. Once

terra firma was established, Venice concentrated on controlling the European leg of the spice and silk trade routes. All new arrivals to the city became potential trading partners and like its signature basilica, Venice was dazzlingly cosmopolitan. So long as everyone was making money, cultural boundaries need not apply.

As a result, by the 15th century, the city was swathed in golden mosaics and rustling silks. La Serenissima (the Most Serene Republic, as Venice was known) kept the peace with a complex system of checks and balances: the Great Council elected the doge while the Consiglio dei Dieci (Council of Ten) thwarted internal political conspiracies and foreign power struggles with a network of spies.

Council of Ten at the Doge's Palace, an illustration by Charles Yriarte

Rehearsal of an Opera,
painting by Marco Ricci

Trendsetters and Troublemakers

As Venice lost ground to the Ottoman Empire and New World trade in the 16th century, the city went on a charm offensive, inspiring an era of art and music. Venice's art was incredibly daring while Venetian music encouraged the mingling of men and women, Italians and foreigners, clergy and socialites.

However, church authorities were not amused by this liberal stance and excommunicated Venice from the Catholic church. In response, in 1767 Venice conducted an audit of the 11 million ducats rendered to Rome in the past decade and promptly closed 127 religious institutions, halving the local clergy and redirecting the funds to state coffers.

Moments in History

452 CE
Refugees from Roman cities on the mainland build on the islets of Rivo Alta (Rialto) and establish the city of Venice.

828
Legend says the corpse of St Mark was smuggled from Alexandria, Egypt. He becomes patron saint.

1470
Venice conquers Cyprus, extending Venetian control from Bergamo to far-flung outposts like Crete and Beirut.

1516
A proclamation declares that Jewish residents of Venice are to live in a designated zone called the Ghetto, with access closed at midnight.

1630
The plague kills a third of Venice's population within 16 months.

1797
Napoléon Bonaparte invades the Veneto; the doge abdicates and the thousand-year Venetian Republic era ends.

1861
Vittorio Emanuele becomes king of Italy; Venice and the Veneto are freed from Austrian rule five years later.

1918
Austro-Hungarian planes drop almost 300 bombs on Venice in WWI, but their aim is mercifully off and little is damaged.

1933
Mussolini inaugurates the Ponte della Libertà from the mainland to Venice. The highway remains the only road link with the mainland.

2024
The 60th edition of the Venice Biennale launches with the theme "Foreigners Everywhere" and is curated by the event's first Latin American curator, Brazilian Adriano Pedrosa.

Party's Over

When Napoléon Bonaparte and his French troops arrived in 1787, Venice had been reduced by plague and circumstance from 175,000 people to 100,000. Ten years later, after being independent for more than a millennium, the Venetian Republic finally fell. It became a pawn in others' battles – the French and Austrians traded the trophy city back and forth – until Napoléon lost in 1814, though not before he'd looted countless masterpieces (still in the Louvre in Paris), lifted restrictions on the Jewish Ghetto and filled in many canals to create wider streets. Venetians hated oppressive Austrian rule and rallied to resist in 1848–49, but were promptly bombed and blockaded. Only Venice's accession to the Kingdom of Italy in 1866 brought them the freedom they craved (the Veneto followed suit four years later).

The city took on an industrial character as the 20th century dawned, its historic port suddenly a feature worth reclaiming. Factories were built on Giudecca and in Cannaregio, and Fascist leader Benito Mussolini added

Representation of Daniele Manin, who led a major revolution in the 19th century

Aerial view of the Grand Canal and Santa Maria Della Salute

a road to the mainland in 1933. During the Second World War, Venice capitulated to Fascism and Allied troops in turn. Postwar, the wartime deportation of the city's historic Jewish population and the flight of many Venetians to other economic centres on the mainland precipitated an urban identity crisis, one only offset by a fast-growing tourism industry.

Venice and the Veneto Today

On 4 November 1966, a new disaster struck as record floods submerged the city. Assistance poured in from admirers around the world who raised $50 million to cover 1,500 restoration projects. Taking fright at future possibilities, in 1973 the Italian state passed a law recognizing the need to maintain the lagoon to safeguard the city. Following suit, in 1987 UNESCO awarded Venice and its lagoon World Heritage Status.

But protecting Venice from floods and a rising influx of tourists has proved a tricky line to tread in an era of mass tourism and global warming. Cue the €5.5 billion MoSE (Modulo Sperimentale Elettromeccanico) flood barrier project, which was signed off in 2003 (since becoming operational in 2020 it has been raised 50 times, successfully protecting the city), and a number of regulations. Large cruise ships were banned from the lagoon in 2021 and, in 2024, the city implemented a fee for and limit on day-trippers during the busiest times of the year.

Despite this progress, the line between living city and floating museum remains a challenging one to navigate. But, what happens in Venice has implications for dozens of other tourist hotspots. This makes the lagoon city more relevant than ever as it seeks a sustainable path between preserving its unique heritage and welcoming the international travellers that have long made this one of the Mediterranean's most admired places.

The MoSE flood barriers, protecting the city

TOP 10
EXPERIENCES

Planning the perfect trip to Venice? Whether you're visiting for the first time or making a return trip, there are some things you simply shouldn't miss out on. To make the most of your time – and to enjoy the very best Venice has to offer – be sure to add these experiences to your list.

1 Tour spectacular Piazza San Marco
Step right into Piazza San Marco *(p30)* and experience its history for yourself: take a tour of Basilica di San Marco *(p22)*, learn Venetian history at Museo Correr *(p32)* and climb the Campanile tower *(p30)* for breathtaking views over the city and lagoon.

2 Explore modern art during the Biennale
Venice is home to the Biennale Art Exhibition *(p80)*, one of the world's biggest platforms for modern art. Works are displayed across the city, with many hosted in places usually closed to the public, giving you a glimpse of secret corners of the city.

3 Get lost in narrow alleys
Create your own tour of Venice's atmospheric *calli* (alleys). They hide a wealth of decorative churches, local markets, artists studios and pretty *campos* (squares). The areas of Santa Croce *(p94)*, San Polo *(p94)* and Dorsoduro *(p100)* offer particularly picturesque local scenes.

4 Bar crawl, Venetian-style
A *giro d'ombra* is Venetian colloquialism slang for "let's grab a drink" and in Venice bar hopping is something of an art form. For the quintessential experience, head to the Rialto market *(p43)* to seek out the most historic bars with the best *cicchetti* (Venetian tapas) since sliced bread.

5 Dine at new-wave gastro osterie

Don't fancy dining in a star-spangled palace hotel? Join the locals at their preferred *osterie* and sample reinvented classic recipes paired with glasses of regional wine. Standouts include Alle Testiere *(p117)* and Estro *(p72)*.

6 Join in Carnival celebrations

Venice's Lent Carnival *(p80)* is a city-wide extravaganza where you'll find masked attendees in coiffed wigs walking the streets. Not here in February? No matter: Venice has a packed calendar, including the Regata Storica boat race *(p81)*.

7 See the city by water

Seeing as Venice's finest views all face outwards towards the canals or the lagoon, board a sleek gondola or water taxi to soak up the scenes. You could even take a few lessons in voga (Venetian standup rowing) with Row Venice *(rowvenice.org)*.

8 Learn centuries-old crafts

Venetians have been renowned for their luxury goods for centuries – even today you can watch ancient techniques used to fashion Murano glass and weave luxurious textiles, and explore your own talents in a workshop with a master.

9 Escape to the Lido

In summer, locals hop on a waterbus at Piazza San Marco to the nearby sandy Lido *(p124)*. Join in with the swimming, cycling or even golfing on a 1920s course – it's a brilliant escape from the city for families with children, too.

10 Discover a mini Rome in Verona

Verona *(p130)* is Roman at heart; after all, they built the triumphal gates and the third largest arena in the world. Sit beneath the stars and listen to the city's renowned opera at the open-air Verona Arena *(p131)*. Bliss.

ITINERARIES

Gliding on a gondola, visiting the mighty Palazzo Ducale, viewing top-tier art: there's a lot to see and do in Venice. With places to eat, drink or simply take in the view, these itineraries offer ways to spend 2 days and 4 days in the city.

2 DAYS

Day 1

Morning
Before there were palaces along the Grand Canal, there was the Pescheria (fish market, *p42*), which is still in full swing today. It's set along a section of the Grand Canal in San Polo, along with a fresh produce market; start your day early here to take in the colourful fish and feathery raddichio, before joining the locals at Al Mercà *(Campo Bella Vienna 213)* for a quick bite. Cross Antonio da Ponte's iconic Rialto Bridge *(p64)*, which offers picturesque views of the Grand Canal, then delve into the narrow lanes and find your way to the Palazzo Contarini del Bovolo *(p89)*. Aim to spend around half an hour here, and make sure you scale its spiral Gothic staircase. If you have time, take the short walk to Museo Fortuny *(p88)*, a gorgeous palace-museum and one-time home of fashion legend Mario Fortuny.

Afternoon
Enjoy a late lunch in sunny Campo Santo Stefano at the popular Le Café *(p92)* before spending the afternoon window-shopping along Calle Larga XXII Marzo, dubbed by many as the Bond Street of Venice. At the end of the street, you'll drop out into Piazza San Marco *(p30)*. Pause for a respite at historic Florian *(p30)*, the world's first café and an architectural jewel, or press on to the award-winning Trattoria Do Forni *(p93)* for dinner. End the day with an exclusive guided night tour of Basilica San Marco *(p22)*, and admire its shimmering gold mosaic and jewel-encrusted altar.

Day 2

Morning
After breakfast, spend your morning on a tour of Venice's political powerhouse, Palazzo Ducale *(p26)*. This Gothic structure was home to Venice's government for nearly seven centuries. It's withstood

> 🍵 **DRINK**
> Located on Calle Vallaresso, opposite the vaporetto stop, you'll find the iconic 1930s Harry's Bar *(p35)*. Take a seat and order a peach Bellini, which it invented. It consists of sparkling prosecco and white peach purée.

The winding staircase at Palazzo Contarini del Bovolo

SHOP
Between the big brand names, look out for home-grown Fortuny, where you'll find gorgeous items like crushed silk velvet scarves and hand-stamped velvet bags, which make for wonderful gifts.

wars, conspiracies and economic crashes. The tour takes you up the Giant's Staircase to the lavish apartments of the Doge, the vast Grand Council Hall and more. Next, make your way to the San Marco Vallaresso vaporetto stop and cross the Grand Canal to Dorsoduro. Disembark at the Accademia stop and wander along alleyways until you reach the San Trovaso canal.

Art for sale in front of the Chiesa di Santa Maria del Giglio

Afternoon
The canalside walk leads you to Cantine del Vino già Schiavi (p72), where you can lunch on delicious *cicchetti* (tapas). Then it's time to lose yourself in the incredible

Peggy Guggenheim Collection (p48), a fine display of the American heiress's outstanding modern art collection, including works by Max Ernst, Pablo Picasso and Salvador Dalí. Back at the vaporetto stop, hop across the Grand Canal to the Chiesa di Santa Maria del Giglio (p89). Around the corner lies the Gritti Palace (p148) where you can reward yourself with dinner at its Bar Longhi.

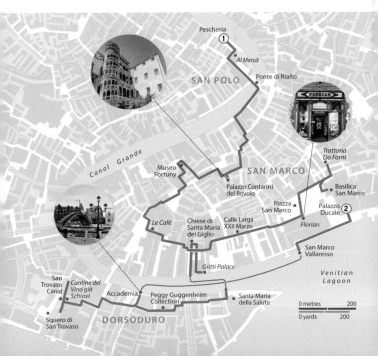

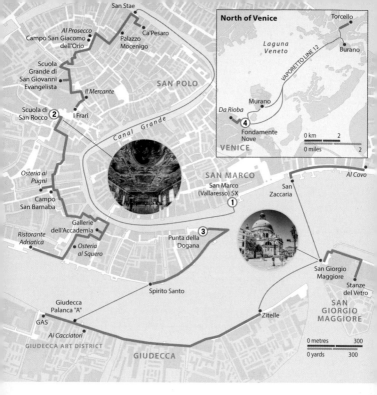

San Stae
Al Prosecco
Campo San Giacomo
dell'Orio
Ca'Pesaro
Palazzo
Mocenigo
Palazzo
Mocenigo
Scuola
Grande di
San Giovanni
Evangelista
Il Mercante
SAN POLO
Scuola di
San Rocco ②
I Frari
Canal Grande
Osteria ai
Pugni
Campo
San Barnaba
Gallerie
dell'Accademia
SAN MARCO
Ristorante
Adriatica
Osteria
al Squero
Punta della
Dogana
San Marco
(Vallaresso) SX ①
San
Zaccaria
③
Al Covo
Giudecca
Palanca "A"
Spirito Santo
San Giorgio
Maggiore
Stanze
del Vetro
GAS
Ai Cacciatori
GIUDECCA ART DISTRICT
GIUDECCA
Zitelle
SAN
GIORGIO
MAGGIORE

North of Venice
Torcello
Laguna
Veneto
VAPORETTO LINE 12
Burano
Murano
Da Rioba
④
Fondamente
Nove
VENICE

0 km   2
0 miles   2

0 metres   300
0 yards   300

4 DAYS

Day 1

Start your four-day tour in style with a cruise along the Grand Canal. Disembark at San Stae and tour Ca' Pesaro (p63), a palazzo-turned-art-museum that houses Venice's modernist masterpieces. Walk to leafy Campo San Giacomo dall'Orio (p95) and lunch at Al Prosecco (p97) on platters of charcuterie and seafood before continuing to Scuola Grande di San Giovanni Evangelista (p96); the 18th-century hall is decorated

The 9th-century church on Campo San Giacomo dall'Orio

with grandiose canvases. Around the corner lies 14th-century I Frari (p40), where you can admire Titian's Assumption altarpiece. Afterwards, hop across a small bridge to Il Mercante (2564 Fondamenta Frari) for cocktails before dinner at a nearby canalside restaurant.

 EAT
Al Gatto Nero (p123) on Burano serves some of the city's best seafood – think Venetian-style cuttlefish – as well as multi-course menus. Beloved by locals, it's a great lunch spot.

> **VIEW**
> There's no denying the beautiful views of the San Marco skyline from the campanile of San Giorgio Maggiore (p54) – the mosaics inside the basilica are just as stunning,, too.

Day 2

Spend a few hours at the Scuola Grande di San Rocco (p95); the church was decorated during the plague by Tintoretto, who painted the interior with 50 captivating scenes of despair and redemption. A five-minute walk brings you to Campo San Barnaba, where you can enjoy a lunch of charcuterie and homemade pasta at Osteria ai Pugni (2836 Fondamenta Gherardini). Your next stop is Gallerie dell'Accademia (p28), Venice's premiere art gallery packed with masterpieces by the likes of Giovanni Bellini, Titian and Tintoretto. Ready to relax? Sip a spritz at canalside Osteria al Squero (943 Dorsoduro), which overlooks one of the last working gondola work-shops in Venice, before ending your day with a swanky dinner at Ristorante Adriatica (palazzoexperimental.com).

Day 3

Begin at the Punta della Dogana (p102), an old customs warehouse that today showcases contemporary art install-ations from billionaire François Pinault's collection, including works by Damien Hirst. Then, take a vaporetto to the residential island of Giudecca (p125) and check out small galleries in the Giudecca Art District (gad-giudeccaart district.com). Take a break at traditional Ai Cacciatori (p129) for bigoli pasta with duck ragu before boarding the vapor-etto at Zitelle to the adjacent island of San Giorgio Maggiore (p126), which is occupied entirely by a huge basilica and monastery. Climb up the campanile to

savour lovely views back across the water to Piazza San Marco. Behind the basilica sits the Stanze del Vetro, a fantastic glass museum showcasing the finest historic and contemporary glasswork. Afterwards, catch the vaporetto back to San Zaccaria and wind down with a fabulous seafood dinner at Al Covo (ristorantealcovo.com).

Day 4

Rise early for a day of island-hopping. From the Fondamente Nove vaporetto stop, visit the islands of the northern lagoon; first up is Torcello (p44), where the first Venetian settlement was established. What remains is the mosaic-adorned Basilica of Santa Maria Assunta. Take a 15-minute vaporetto ride south to Burano (p120). Spend an hour or two here, where you can visit the beautifully curated Lace Museum (p63) and enjoy a fine lunch at Al Gatto Nero (p123). Once you're ready, board the vaporetto to Murano (p121) and make a beeline to the Glass Museum (p121) to understand the background and history of the craft. Rest your feet on the 30-minute vaporetto ride back to Fondamente Nove and find your way to Da Rioba (p111), which gives modern twists to its fish-based dishes.

Colourful houses lining the canal on the small island of Burano

TOP 10 HIGHLIGHTS

Basilica di San Marco

EXPLORE THE
HIGHLIGHTS

There are some sights in Venice you simply shouldn't miss, and it's these attractions that make the Top 10. Discover what makes each one a must-see on the following pages.

Ponte degi Scalzi

CAMPO S. SIMEON PROFETA

CAMPO NAZARIO SAURO

Canal Grande

SANTA CROCE

CAMPO SAN STIN

FMTA MINOTTO

6 CAMPO DEI FRARI

CAMPO SAN PANTALON

9

CAMPO SAN BARNABA

DORSODURO

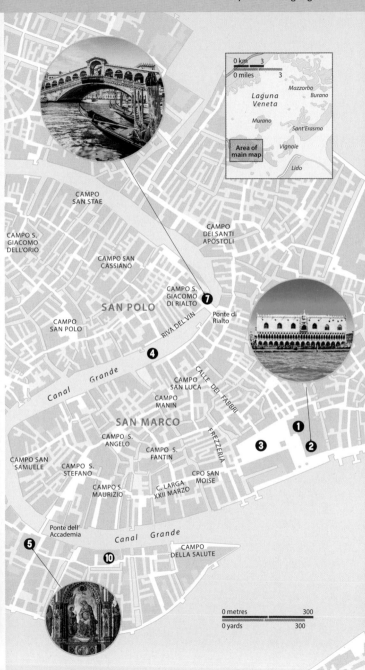

0 km   3
0 miles   3

*Laguna
Veneta*

Mazzorbo
Burano

Murano

Sant'Erasmo

**Area of
main map**

Vignole

Lido

CAMPO
SAN STAE

CAMPO
DEI SANTI
APOSTOLI

CAMPO S.
GIACOMO
DELL'ORIO

CAMPO SAN
CASSIANO

CAMPO S.
GIACOMO
DI RIALTO   **7**

SAN POLO   Ponte di
                                  Rialto

CAMPO
SAN POLO   RIVA DEL VIN

            4

Canal Grande   CALLE DEL FABBRI

                CAMPO
                SAN LUCA

                CAMPO
                MANIN

        SAN MARCO   **1**

        CAMPO S.   **3**   **2**
        ANGELO
                  CAMPO S.
                  FANTIN   FREZZERIA

CAMPO SAN
SAMUELE   CAMPO S.
            STEFANO
                  CPO SAN
                  MOISE
        CAMPO S.   C. LARGA
        MAURIZIO   XXII MARZO

Ponte dell'
Accademia   Canal Grande

5   CAMPO
        10   DELLA SALUTE

0 metres   300
0 yards   300

1

BASILICA DI SAN MARCO

📍 Q5 🏛 Piazza San Marco 🕐 9:30am–5:15pm Mon–Sat, 2–5:15pm Sun & hols (last adm: 4:45pm) 🌐 basilicasanmarco.it; st-marks-basilica.com (for tour bookings) 🎫 🎧

The breathtaking Byzantine basilica dominating Piazza San Marco was constructed as an embodiment of the Venetian Republic's power and as a fitting resting place for St Mark. Gloriously framed by mosaics, treasures and columns, it is one of Europe's greatest buildings.

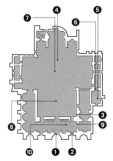

Basilica di San Marco Floorplan

1 Western Façade

A succession of domes, columns, arches and spires, interspersed with statues, screens and glittering mosaics, greets tourists in Piazza San Marco. The north-ernmost arch houses 13th-century mosaics that depict the basilica itself. Other mosaics are copies from the 17th and 18th centuries.

2 Atrium Mosaics

These were created in the Byzantine tradi-tion, and provide detailed accounts of the Old Testament. The 13th-century cupola's concen-tric circles recount 24 episodes from the Book of Genesis, including the Creation. Carry a pair of binoculars to examine the mosaics close-up.

3 Flooring

The elaborate tessellated floors are a mosaic masterpiece made with multicoloured stones on uneven levels, creating a pattern evoca-tive of the sea. Intricate geometrical designs sit alongside striking animal motifs in this unique creation.

TOP TIP

Visit at dusk, when the setting sun lights up the façade.

Façade of the spectacular Basilica di San Marco

The basilica interior with its stunning mosaics

4 Pala d'Oro

The basilica's altarpiece features a jewel-encrusted gold screen, which was commissioned in Constantinople in 976 but added to at later dates. It has 250 panels bearing 1,927 precious gems, and cloisonné plaques. A separate admission fee may be charged to view the retable.

5 The Tetrarchs

The inspiration for these coarse porphyry figures is still unknown. They probably represent the four emperors of the eastern and western Roman empires. The statue was pillaged from Constantinople during the Fourth Crusade in 1204.

6 Treasury

The basilica's glittering riches include precious chalices of rock crystal enamelled by medieval silversmiths and goldsmiths and reliquaries from Venice's eastern conquests, including parts of the True Cross and the throne-reliquary of St Mark. A separate admission fee will apply to visit the treasury.

7 Ascension Dome

The central dome has a spectacular array of early 13th-century mosaics, depicting the New Testament. *Christ in Glory*, along with depictions of the Virtues are featured in the dome.

8 Pentecost Dome

Probably the first dome of the basilica to be adorned with mosaics, the Pentecost depicts the Descent of the Holy Ghost, seen as a flame over the heads of the 12 apostles.

9 Loggia dei Cavalli

The celebrated quartet of bronze horses that once stood here gave this balcony its name. They are now located in the basilica museum. However, the balcony itself is worth visiting for stunning views of Piazza San Marco and Venice. Visitors can also see clutches of columns in various decorative styles.

10 Basilica Museum

🕐 9:45am–5:45pm daily (last adm: 4:45pm) 🔳 Steps from the atrium lead to the basilica's museum. The star exhibit here is the gold-covered quartet of horses stolen during the Fourth Crusade. These restored Graeco-Roman equine figures originally graced the Hippodrome in Constantinople. The museum also displays manuscripts and liturgies.

> ### BUILDING THE BASILICA
>
> Construction of the basilica first began in 829, but it was burned down in 976 in a revolt. The present building dates from 1071, when a grand basilica was built to reflect Venice's growing power. The basilica became the city cathedral in 1807.

A gilded bronze horse in the basilica museum

Basilica Architectural Features

1. Galleries
The airy catwalks over the body of the basilica reflect the eastern tradition of segregation in worship, as they were exclusively for women. They are closed to visitors.

2. Stone Wall Slabs
Brick-faced until the 1100s, the walls of the basilica were then covered with stone slabs from the Near East, sliced lengthways to produce a kaleidoscopic effect.

3. Zen Chapel
The ornate decoration in this chapel was executed for the funeral of its namesake, Cardinal Zen, in 1521, in recognition of his gifts to the state. Open for prayer only.

4. The "Victory Bringer"
This revered Byzantine icon is given pride of place in the Madonna of Nicopeia Chapel. Rumoured to have been executed by St Luke, it was carried into battle for its miraculous powers.

5. Baptistry
Aglow with 14th-century mosaic scenes depicting the life of St John, this is also home to the tomb of Italian architect Jacopo Sansovino (p61). Open for prayer only.

Romanesque sculptures on the façade of the basilica

6. Romanesque Stone Carvings
The exquisite semicircular stone carvings over the central doorway were executed between 1235 and 1265; you can still see traces of them.

7. Iconostasis
This elaborate screen separates the worship area of the chancel from the nave. Atop its eight columns are Gothic-style statues of the Virgin and the apostles, sculpted by the Dalle Masegne brothers in 1394.

8. Byzantine Pierced Screens
Influenced by eastern architecture, the delicate geometrical designs and lattice-work stone screens are featured on all three façades in the atrium and loggia.

9. Porta dei Fiori
This doorway on the northern façade bears a 13th-century nativity scene surrounded by Moorish arches.

10. Altar Columns
Four finely carved alabaster and marble columns support a canopy at the altar, beneath which lies the body of St Mark.

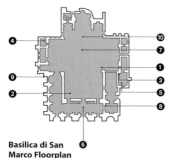
Basilica di San Marco Floorplan

ST MARK, PATRON SAINT OF VENICE

St Mark the Evangelist, patron saint of Venice

Although the well-loved saint of Byzantium St Theodore had been appointed protector of Venice by the Byzantine emperor, the fledgling republic felt in need of a saint of its own. According to legend, in 828 CE, two adroit Venetian merchants filched the relics of St Mark the Evangelist from a monastery in Alexandria, transporting them under layers of pork fat to conceal them from Muslim guards. Their welcome in Venice was triumphant, and the story was recounted in countless paintings and mosaics. The remains, however, were mislaid for years, until one of the saint's arms miraculously broke through a column in 1094 (marked by a small cross, left of the Altar of the Sacrament) in answer to a prayer. St Mark now rests in peace beneath the basilica's main altar. The ubiquitous winged lion representing St Mark could be found throughout the republic as the trademark of Venetian dominion: it is often shown with two paws in the sea and two on land, to symbolize the geography of Venice.

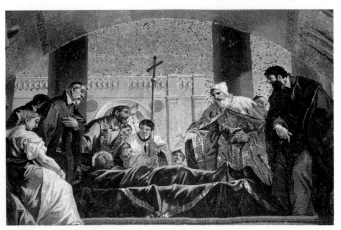

Basilica mosaic depicting St Mark's body venerated by the Doge

2

DOGE'S PALACE

📍 R5 🏛 Piazza San Marco 🕐 9am–7pm daily (Nov–Mar: to 6pm); 6 Jan, 9, 10 & 23 Dec: 9am–9pm (last adm: 1 hour before closing) 🌐 visitmuve.it 📷📱

A masterpiece of Byzantine, Gothic and Renaissance architecture, the Palazzo Ducale (Doge's Palace) was the official residence of the 120 doges who ruled Venice from 697 to 1797. Artists such as Titian, Tintoretto and Bellini, not to mention architects Antonio Rizzo and Pietro Lombardo, embellished the palace with painting and sculpture.

1 Façade

Elegant twin façades face the piazzetta and the quayside. Pink-and-cream stonework and a loggia stand above an arcade of columns. These columns feature 36 intricately sculpted Istrian stone capitals.

2 Prisons

A fascinating maze of cells is linked by corridors and stair-cases on both sides of the canal. One of the most famous inmates, Casanova (p56), made a dramatic escape across the roof in 1756. The "new prisons" were in use until the 1940s and feature poignant graffiti by internees.

3 Armoury

This is a gripping, if spine-chilling, collection of beautifully crafted firearms, ceremonial weapons and suits of armour from Asia and the West. Among the war trophies

> **TOP TIP**
>
> On the ground floor, the Museo dell'Opera displays the palace's façade capitals.

The Doge's Palace, a UNESCO World Heritage Site

is a Turkish standard brought back from the Battle of Lepanto (1571).

4 Sala del Senato
Senate members met in this lavish hall decorated with ceiling frescoes to debate war, foreign affairs and trade with the Doge. Time was measured using two clocks – one with a 24-hour face and the other with zodiac signs.

5 Bridge of Sighs
One of the world's most famous bridges, the Ponte dei Sospiri is an early 17th-century Baroque structure that crosses the palace prisons. The condemned would "sigh" at their last glimpse of sky and sea while crossing this bridge.

6 Sala dello Scudo
Enormous globes and painted wall maps showing the known world in 1762 make this room a must. The map of Eastern Asia traces Marco Polo's travels to China, complete with documentation

Superb frescoes in the Sala del Senato

of species of flora and fauna still unknown in the West then.

7 Scala d'Oro
The magnificent Golden Staircase, so-called for its Classical stucco decorations in 24-carat gold-leaf framing frescoes, led guests of honour to the second floor. Designed by Sansovino *(p61)*, it was later completed by Scarpagnino in 1559.

8 Sala del Maggior Consiglio
The Great Council Chamber is lined with canvases of Venetian victories and a cornice frieze of 76 doges. A black curtain represents traitor Marin Faliero *(p29)*, who led a coup against the ruling patricians in the 14th century.

9 Doge's Apartments
The rooms of the Doge's living quarters

include rich brocades, manuscripts, triumphal friezes, gilded ceilings and works of art.

10 Porta della Carta
The palace's main entrance, which is now the visitors' exit, has a beautifully sculpted 1438 portal by the Bon family. The name "paper door" arose because edicts were posted here.

THE GREAT COUNCIL

By the mid-16th century the Great Council had increased to around 2,000 members. Any Venetian of high birth over 25 years old was entitled to a seat – with the exception of those married to a commoner. From 1646, merchants could purchase a seat with 100,000 ducats.

A giant globe in the Sala dello Scudo

Doge's Palace
Art and Architecture

1. Paradise
Possibly the world's largest oil painting (1588–90), *Paradise* by Jacopo and Domenico Tintoretto is said to contain 800 figures. It's housed in the Sala del Maggior Consiglio.

2. Arcade Capital
Proclaimed the "most beautiful in Europe" by art critic John Ruskin, this eight-sided carved capital on the southwest corner of the palace shows the zodiac signs and planets in imaginative detail.

3. Giants' Staircase
This staircase is so named for its two colossal statues of Mars and Neptune, which were sculpted by Sansovino in 1567 as symbols of Venice's power. Visiting dignitaries would ascend the marble-lined stairs to the palace.

4. Drunkenness of Noah
A powerful sculpture from the early 15th century adorns the façade's southeast corner. Noah, inebriated and half-naked before his sons, is intended to portray the weakness of man.

Veronese's *Rape of Europa*, one of the most eye-catching works in the palace

5. Rape of Europa
Veronese's allegorical work (1580) in the Anticollegio shows Europa sitting on a bull.

6. The Triumph of Venice
Dominating the Sala del Senato is Tintoretto's glorious work (1580–84), showing allegorical figures proffering fruits of the sea to Venice.

7. Central Balcony
This magnificent early 15th-century stone terrace, embellished with columns and spires, opens off the Sala del Maggior Consiglio with a breathtaking view of the lagoon.

8. Arco Foscari
This triumphal archway of pink-and-cream stone layers leading to the Giants' Staircase was commissioned by Doge Foscari in 1438.

9. Wellheads
Elaborate 16th-century wellheads were constructed to drain water from the gutters to the palace's central courtyard.

10. Coronation of the Virgin
The remains of Guariento's fresco, discovered beneath Tintoretto's *Paradise*, are housed in a side room, with panels detailing its restoration.

The *Drunkenness of Noah* sculpture on the corner of the palace

THE EXTENT OF THE VENETIAN REPUBLIC

In its earliest days, Venice was little more than a huddle of islands in the middle of a shallow marshy lagoon, settled by a band of refugees from the Veneto region. Yet over the centuries it developed into a mighty republic reaching south to the Mediterranean and north to the Alps – primarily by establishing itself as a vital centre for trade and commerce. Salt was stored in massive warehouses, there were dealings in spices and fabrics from the East, crusades were organized and fitted out here, and relics procured. It was in the 15th and 16th centuries that the Venetian empire reached its zenith, having colonized all of Northeastern Italy and secured a monopoly on Mediterranean trade. Its main population probably never exceeded 160,000. However, well beyond its walled port towns, which stretched down the Dalmatian coast, were far-flung outposts such as Crete and Cyprus. These dominions protected key trading routes (between Venice and Arabic countries). Westwards across the Po plain, Venice's influence took in Treviso, Vicenza and Verona, extending to Bergamo on the outskirts of Milan and the mighty Visconti dynasty.

Veronese's *The Victorious Return of Doge Andrea Contarini after the Triumph in Chioggia*, and *(left)* Venetian and Genoese fleets during the naval battle of Chioggia

3

PIAZZA SAN MARCO

📍 Q5

Long the political and religious heart of Venice, Piazza San Marco was once just a monastery garden. The glittering basilica and Doge's Palace command the east side of the square, while other stately buildings along its borders have been the backdrop for magnificent processions. Today the piazza continues to thrive with a museum complex and cafés.

> ☕ **DRINK**
> Grab a delicious cup of coffee al fresco at one of the cafés and let San Marco's colonnaded grandeur wash over you.

1 Doge's Palace

The designers of the Doge's residence (p26) broke with tradition by perching the bulk of the pink Veronese marble palace on lace-like Istrian stone arcades, with a portico supported by columns below.

2 Giardinetti Reali

These public gardens, created during the Napoleonic era, took the place of boatyards and grain stores, situated just behind the waterfront.

3 Campanile

🕐 9:30am–9:15pm daily (last adm: 8:45pm)
🌐 venetoinside.com ⚡

Views of the city and lagoon can be had by taking the elevator to the top of this 98-m (323-ft) bell tower. It was masterfully rebuilt to its 16th-century design following its clamorous collapse in 1902. Book guided tours online.

4 Caffè Florian

🌐 caffeflorian.com

Reputedly Europe's first coffee house, the

Historic Caffè Florian in the heart of the piazza

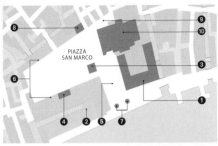

The campanile dominating Piazza San Marco

premises still retain their original 1720 wood-panelling, marble-topped tables and gilt-framed mirrors.

5 Piazzetta

Once an inlet for boats and witness to the arrival of distinguished visitors during the Republic's heyday, this now fully paved mini square fronts the lagoon.

6 Procuratie Vecchie and Nuove

The Procurators, who were responsible for state administration, lived in these elegant buildings.

7 Column of San Marco

This is one of two granite columns erected in 1172 by Nicolò Barattieri; the other symbolizes San Teodoro. Public executions were held here.

8 Torre dell'Orologio

⏰ Hours vary, chech website ▦ muve. vivaticket.it

This Renaissance-style clock tower is topped by two bronze Moors hammering out the hours on the upper terrace. At Epiphany and Ascension there is an hourly procession of clockwork Magi that are led by an angel. Book guided tours online.

9 Piazzetta dei Leoncini

This is the site of a former vegetable market, where a pair of small lions (leoncini) carved from red Verona stone have been crouching since 1722.

10 Basilica di San Marco

This Byzantine structure (p22) dominates the eastern side of Piazza San Marco. Its exterior features pointed arches and huge domes, while the interior has mosaic floors and artifacts.

The Torre dell'Orologio clock tower in the piazza

VENICE'S BELLS

Booming through the city, the five bells in the Campanile have been employed to mark Venice's rhythms for centuries. The Maleficio bell was sounded to announce an execution, the Nona rang at midday, the Trottiera spurred on the nobles' horses for assemblies in the Doge's Palace and the Mezza Terza was used to indicate that the Senate was in session. The Marangona bell is still sounded to mark midnight.

Museo Correr Complex

1. Biblioteca Marciana Ceiling
The ceiling vault of the opulent reading room (one of the *sale monumentali*), inside the Libreria Sansoviniana, collapsed in 1545. The architect Sansovino was held responsible for this and imprisoned – he was later released to complete the job at his own expense. Titian selected artists for the decorations; Veronese was awarded a gold chain for the best work.

2. Libreria Sansoviniana Staircase
Bedecked with gilt and stucco decorations by Alessandro Vittoria, the 16th-century staircase leads from a monumental entrance on the piazza to the halls of the old library.

3. Veneziano Paintings
This prolific Byzantine artist is featured in the Pinacoteca's Room 25 (part of Museo Correr), with glowing two-dimensional religious portraits (1290–1302).

4. Correr Ballroom
This Neo-Classical creation was built for Napoleon. It is now used for exhibitions.

5. Canova Statues
In the Museo Correr, works by Antonio Canova (1767–1822), foremost sculptor of his time, include his acclaimed statues of Orpheus and Eurydice.

6. Two Venetian Ladies
Carpaccio's masterpiece of well-dressed ladies (1500–10) is in Room 38 of the Museo Correr.

Canova's statue of Orpheus

Grandiose ceiling of the reading room at the Biblioteca Marciana

It was first thought to depict courtesans because of the ladies' décolleté dresses, but the women are, in fact, awaiting their menfolk's return from hunting.

7. Map of Venice
The place of pride in Room 22 of the Museo Correr goes to Jacopo de' Barbari's prospective map-layout of Venice (1497–1500), which was painstakingly engraved on six pear-wood panels.

8. Bellini Room
Works by the talented Bellini family are on display in Room 36 of the Pinacoteca: the poignant *Dead Christ Supported by Two Angels* (1453–5) by the best known, Giovanni; head of the family Jacopo's *Crucifixion* (1450); and son Gentile's portrait of *Doge Giovanni Mocenigo* (1475).

9. The Royal Rooms
Consisting of 20 rooms, the Royal Rooms were once the apartments of archdukes, kings and emperors who passed through Venice in the 19th century. They were mainly from three ruling houses: Bonaparte, Habsburgs and Savoy.

10. Crafts and Guilds
Wooden sandals 60-cm (24-inches) high, inlaid with mother-of-pearl, illustrate the stiff demands put upon followers of 15th- to 17th-century fashion (Room 48).

ACQUA ALTA FLOODING

A trestle bridge set up in the piazza during Venice's *acqua alta*

Acqua alta ("high water") has long been disruptive to the city between October and March. However, it has also become unpredictable with time. Venice and its lagoon are subject to the tides of the Adriatic Sea but flood levels are caused by the coincidence of low atmospheric pressure, strong sirocco winds from the south and natural high tides due to moon phases. As warning sirens fill the air, people drag out their waterproof boots, shop-keepers rush to put up barriers and street-sweepers lay out duck-boards in low-lying spots. The lowest points of the city, including the area along the Grand Canal and Piazza San Marco, face a disruption in daily activities and incur low footfall. Being very close to the waters of the lagoon, Piazza San Marco is one of the most vulnerable spots. People have to make use of the elevated walkways until the water drains out, which can take a few hours. The flood gates designed for the Lido sea entrances are held by many experts to be both useless and harmful to the lagoon. However, there are plans for a drainage system on the piazza, dredging canals and raising paving levels.

A flooded Piazza San Marco after a high tide

4

GRAND CANAL

Venice's majestic "highway", the Canal Grande, is only one of the 177 canals flowing through the city, but covering over 4 km (2.5 miles), it certainly earns its name. The river snakes through the city with a double curve, its banks lined with exquisite palaces, displaying some of the finest architecture of the Republic. On its waters, colourful flotillas of gondolas, ferries, taxi launches, high-speed police boats and barges packed with fresh produce provide endless fascination.

1 Fondaco dei Turchi

With an ornate air and its characteristic round arches, this Veneto-Byzantine building, dating from 1225, was the Turkish trade centre for 200 years. It now houses the Museo di Storia Naturale (p132).

2 Rialto Bridge

One of the city's most familiar sights (p64), the striking 28-m- (92-ft) wide, 8-m- (26-ft-) high Istrian stone Ponte di Rialto dates from 1588.

3 Riva del Vin

A sunny quayside with a string of open-air restaurants, this is one of the few accessible banks of the Grand Canal. Barrels of *vino* (wine) used to be off-loaded here, hence the name.

4 Ca' Rezzonico

The finest feature of this palace (p53) is its grand staircase. Today it houses a museum of 18th-century Venice.

5 Ca' Dario

With an ornamental Renaissance façade studded with a number of colourful stone medallions, this lopsided palace (p52) is supposedly cursed owing to the many misfortunes that have overtaken its various owners.

Galleria Internazionale d'Arte Moderna, Ca' Pesaro

6 Accademia Bridge

The lovely wooden Ponte dell'Accademia, built in 1932 by the engineer Miozzi, was intended as a temporary measure until a more substantial structure was designed, but it is now a permanent fixture. It affords stunning views of the Grand Canal.

7 Ca' Pesaro

This colossal Baroque palace (p97), decorated with diamond-point ashlar work, was the final creation of renowned Venetian architect Baldassare Longhena. Home to the city's modern art collections, it is beautifully floodlit at night.

The wooden Accademia Bridge

Santa Maria della Salute on the Grand Canal

WAVE DAMAGE

Damage to buildings caused by wash has worsened with the rise in motor-propelled craft. Waves provoked by boats eat into foundations on the water's edge. Speed limits aim to curb this: 7-11 kmph (4.5-7 mph) on the Grand Canal; 5 kmph (3 mph) on narrower canals; and 20 kmph (12.5 mph) on the lagoon.

8 Santa Maria della Salute

Longhena's 17th-century Baroque masterpiece features sculpted whorls beneath a towering dome. This church (p54) was commissioned to commemorate the end of a devastating plague in the city.

9 Harry's Bar

The famed watering hole (p89) of author Ernest Hemingway is where the Bellini aperitivo was invented. Opened in 1931 by Arrigo Cipriani, it was named after the American who funded it.

10 Punta della Dogana

The figure of Fortune stands atop the erstwhile customs house, now an arts centre (p102), and doubles as a weather vane. A gilded globe held by two Atlas figures supports her. This is where the Grand Canal joins St Mark's Basin.

VIEW

Take the vaporetto Line 1 for an hour-long ride with the best views of the sights along the canal.

Striking sculpture on top of Punta della Dogana

Watercraft of Venice

1. Gondola
These boats are most often seen transporting tourists around the canals. A larger version, called the *traghetto*, is also used for the cross-canal ferry *(p43)*, while the smaller *gondolino* is a slender racing craft.

2. Vaporetto
This is the capacious rounded waterbus, now also seen in an "eco-logical" electric model. A slimmer *motoscafo* serves the outer runs and narrow canals with lower bridges.

3. Sandolo
This slim, lightweight boat is suited to hunting and fishing in the lagoon's shallow waters, and for racing. Painted black, these "imitation gondolas" can deceive tourists on the back canals.

4. Topo
The most commonly used barge for transporting goods around the canals, the *topo* can be seen loaded with everything from demijohns to washing machines, often with a live dog "figurehead" on the prow.

5. Fire Boat
From their station near Ca' Foscari, the red launches are called both to deal with fires and to rescue submerged obstacles and crumbling façades.

A car ferry on the Grand Canal transporting passengers and vehicles

6. Car Ferry
These giants convey all manner of motor vehicles from the Tronchetto to the Lido. Passengers can even carry their bicycles, which are a convenient way to navigate the city's narrow roads.

7. Sanpierota
This flat-bottomed rowing boat is named after the inhabitants of San Pietro in Volta *(p127)* in the southern lagoon. Once used for transporting fish to Venice, nowadays it is fitted with an outboard motor and photo-genic oblique sail.

8. Garbage Vessel
The city's hefty waste-collecting AMAV barges trundle over the lagoon with the day's rubbish. In addition, they also undertake essential environmen-tal monitoring.

9. Ambulance and Police Launches
These modern craft attract plenty of attention as they thunder down the canals – only the emergency categories are allowed to disregard the city's speed limits.

10. Bragozzo
With its gently rounded prow and stern, this brightly coloured two-masted sailing boat was traditionally used for fishing by the inhabitants of Chioggia *(p127)* and can still be seen near the islands.

Firefighters navigating a narrow canal in a fire boat

VENICE'S GONDOLAS

The quintessential sleek Venetian gondola has been plying the city's canals since as early as the 11th century, although it did not take on its present graceful form until the late 1400s. Compared to a mere 405 gondolas on the waterways today, as many as 10,000 were in use in the late 19th century. Bridges were fewer in number then and located far away from each other – gondolas acted as ferries between one island and another, a custom that continues to this day across the Grand Canal by the *traghetti*. A handful of gondola yards still construct the boats as well as carry out repairs, such as San Trovaso in Dorsoduro. It's a costly and complex craft – eight different types of wood and a heavy iron bracket *(ferro)* are needed for a total of 280 pieces to make the asymmetrical craft, 11 m (36 ft) in length and 1.42 m (4.5 ft) in width, at a cost approaching €25,000. Originally painted in bright colours, the black gondolas seen today were decreed by the Senate to prevent excessive shows of wealth. Used almost exclusively by tourists now, gondolas are undeniably the most romantic way to see the city.

A crafter at work making *fórcolas* (the Venetian rowlock used to hold the oar) for gondolas

Riding in Venice's traditional wooden gondolas

ACCADEMIA GALLERIES

📍 M6 🏛 Campo della Carità, Dorsoduro 1050 🕐 8:15am–2pm Mon, 8:15am–7:15pm Tue–Sun (last adm: 1 hour before closing time) 🚫 1 Jan, 1 May, 25 Dec 🌐 gallerieaccademia.it 📱

Occupying three former religious establishments, the Gallerie dell'Accademia is Venice's answer to the Uffizi in Florence. It hosts a great collection of masterpieces spanning the development of Venetian art from Byzantine and Renaissance to Baroque and Rococo.

1 Portrait of a Gentleman

Lorenzo Lotto's sombre image of a melancholic man of means in his study (1528) may have been a self-portrait (Room XIII). Lotto was known for works of psychological insight.

2 The Tempest

This enigmatic 1506 portrayal of a woman suckling her child is by Giorgione (Room VIII). The overall impression is of the figures and the dream-like, stormy landscape blended into one whole.

Bellini's vivid *Procession in St Mark's Square*

VIEW
📷 The paintings in the Accademia Galleries depend on natural light. For the best viewing, plan a visit on a bright, sunny morning.

3 Pietà

Titian's last work (1576) is unfinished but it is also considered his best (Room XI). Painted during the plague, the *Pietà* is imbued with golden light and a piercing sense of anguish.

4 Procession in St Mark's Square

This canvas is a part of Gentile Bellini's spectacular cycle (1496) of the St Mark's Day procession in 1444. It can be seen in Room XX.

GALLERY GUIDE
The vast gallery is organized in chronological order for the most part. All the rooms are clearly labelled with roman numerals and have explanatory cards in English. The Quadreria corridor, filled with masterpieces, is noteworthy.

5 Feast in the House of Levi

The forceful canvas by Veronese (1573) occupies an entire wall in Room X. It was the source of much controversy in its time – the church authorities, who commissioned it as "The Last Supper", were angered by the inclusion of "dogs, buffoons, drunken Germans, dwarfs and other such absurdities" in the painting – so Veronese changed the title.

6 Meeting and Departure of the Betrothed Ursula and Ereo

The largest painting in Carpaccio's magnificent four-canvas narrative cycle (1495) about a Breton princess and an English prince can be seen in Room XXI.

7 Madonna dell'Arancio

This exquisite work (1496–8) by Cima da Conegliano, painted for a Murano Franciscan church, is enlivened with partridges and plant life, all infused with allegorical meaning (Room II).

8 Coronation of the Virgin

This resplendent polyptych (1350) by Venice's leading 14th-century artist, Paolo Veneziano, is the first work in Room I. Flanking the stunning Byzantine-inspired central piece are events depicted from the life of Christ.

9 San Giobbe Altarpiece

Bellini's inspirational altarpiece (Room II) was painted in 1487 for the Church of San Giobbe. It is regarded as one of the finest examples of the Sacra Conversazione, which was central to 15th-century Venetian art. The pre-sence of St Sebastian and St Giobbe beside

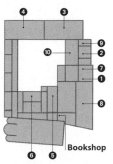

Accademia Galleries Flooplan

the Virgin suggests the aftermath of plague, while angel musicians pay homage to San Giobbe, patron saint of music.

Giovanni Bellini's altarpiece for San Giobbe

10 Lion of St Mark with Saints John the Baptist, John the Evangelist, Mary Magdalene and Jerome

Remarkable for its serenity, this marvellous canvas by Cima di Conegliano depicts a winged lion flanked by four saints (Room VIb).

Feast in the House of Levi by Paolo Veronese

SANTA MARIA GLORIOSA DEI FRARI

📍 L3 🏛 Campo dei Frari, San Polo 🕐 9am–6pm Mon–Sat, 1–6pm Sun
(last adm: 30 min before closing) 🚫 1 Jan, Easter, 15 Aug, 25 Dec
🌐 chorusvenezia.org; basilicadeifrari.it 🔗

A masterpiece of Venetian Gothic ecclesiastical architecture, this cavernous 15th-century Franciscan church houses canvases by the likes of Titian and Bellini, along with tombs of doges and artists.

1 Rood Screen
This beautiful screen, which divides the worship area and nave is carved in a blend of Renaissance and Gothic styles by Pietro Lombardo and Bartolomeo Bon (1475). It is also decorated with marble figures.

2 Choir Stalls
Unique in Venice, the original three tiers of 124 friars' seats deserve close examination for their inlaid woodwork. Crafted by Marco Cozzi in 1468, the stalls demonstrate the influence of late Gothic, Classical and Venetian styles.

3 Madonna Enthroned with Saints
Tucked away in the sacristy, and still in its original engraved frame, is another delight for Bellini fans (1488). "It seems painted with molten gems," wrote author Henry James of the triptych.

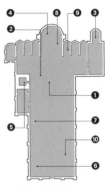

Santa Maria Gloriosa dei Frari Floorplan

The Frari's 12 pillars, symbolizing the apostles

4 Assumption of the Virgin
Titian's glowing 1518 depiction of the triumphant ascent of Mary shows her robed in

Ornate three-tiered choir stalls with carvings

crimson accompanied by a semicircle of saints, while the 12 apostles are left gesticulating in wonderment below. This brilliant canvas hangs over the high altar and is the inevitable focus of the church.

Gothic façade of Santa Maria Gloriosa dei Frari

5 Campanile

The robust bell tower set into the church's left transept was built in the 14th century and is the second tallest in Venice.

6 Canova's Mausoleum

This colossal pyramidal monument is based on Canova's Neo-Classical

design for Titian's tomb. Though not realized during Canova's lifetime, it was completed in 1822 by five of his students as a tribute to him.

7 Mausoleum of Doge Giovanni Pesaro

The monsters and black marble figures supporting the sarcophagus of this macabre Baroque monument prompted art critic John Ruskin to write "it seems impossible for false taste and base feeling to sink lower".

8 Monument to Doge Francesco Foscari

This is a fine Renaissance tribute to the man responsible for Venice's mainland expansion. Foscari was the subject of Lord Byron's *The Two Foscari*, which was turned into an opera by Verdi.

9 Statue of John the Baptist

The inspirational wood statue of John the Baptist from 1450, which was created especially

> **VIEW**
> At Christmas, you can enjoy the nativity scene at the church with lighting effects and lifelike moving figures.

for the church by artist Donatello (1386–1466), stands in the Florentine chapel. The striking emaciated carved figure is renowned for being particularly lifelike.

10 Monument to Titian

Titian was afforded special authorization for burial here after his death during the 1576 plague, although this sturdy mausoleum was not built for another 300 years. A statue of Titian wearing a laurel crown stands in the centre.

Memorial to Titian inside the church

STATE ARCHIVES

The labyrinthine monastery and courtyards near the church have been home to Venice's State Archives since the Republic's fall. Its 300 rooms and 70 km (43 miles) of shelves are filled with records on the history of Venice from the 9th century onwards, including the Golden Book register of the Venetian aristocracy. Scholars enter via the Oratorio di San Nicolò della Lattuga (1332), named after the miraculous recovery of a Procurator of San Marco thanks to the healing qualities of a lettuce (*lattuga*).

THE RIALTO

🔲 P2 🏠 San Polo

The commercial hub and historical heart of Venice, the Rialto is as bustling today as it has always been – records tell of markets here since 1097. A few 16th-century buildings also survive, and add to the charm of the area. Today, locals and visitors alike shop at the colourful market stalls and gather on the Rialto Bridge to watch the gondolas glide on the Grand Canal.

1 Fresh Produce Market

⏱ 7:30am–8pm Mon–Sat

The market here offers luscious peaches and cherries, thorny artichokes and red chicory from Treviso. Fruit, vegetables and fish are strictly seasonal.

2 Pescheria

⏱ 7:30am–2pm Tue–Sat

Writhing eels, huge swordfish, soft-shelled crabs and crimson-fleshed fresh tuna are among the stars of the 1907 Neo-Gothic fish market hall, which is barely out of reach of the scavenging seagulls.

3 San Giacomo di Rialto

The oldest church in Venice claims to have a foundation set by a pious carpenter in the 5th century, although the present building is medieval.

> 🍴 **EAT**
> In addition to fresh fruit from the market, picnic supplies can be bought at the delicatessens and bakeries in the neighbourhood.

The Gothic portico, with a Latin cross and central dome, as well as the huge 24-hour clock are well worth a look.

Clockwise from far left **Fresh produce at the market; church of San Giacomo di Rialto; Palazzo dei Camerlenghi along the Grand Canal; marble statue of** *Il Gobbo di Rialto*

Looking down the Grand Canal from Rialto Bridge

4 Public Rostrum

New laws and names of criminals were announced from atop this porphyry column, supported by a stone figure known as *il gobbo* (hunchback).

5 Palazzo dei Camerlenghi

This lopsided 1525 palace once imprisoned debtors on the ground floor, while the top floors served as offices for the city *camerlenghi* (treasurers).

6 Gondola Ferry

A must for every visitor is a trip on the *traghetto* ferry across the Grand Canal – one of only eight still in operation. Custom dictates that passengers should remain standing.

7 Banco Giro Arcade

Merchants from the East and the West gathered to exchange a variety of goods, including silks and spices, outside the city's first bank set up in 1157, which is now a wine bar.

8 Ruga degli Orefici

This lovely covered passageway decorated with frescoes has been home to silversmiths, goldsmiths and silk traders since the 1300s.

9 Fabbriche Nuove

Uniformed *carabinieri* (police) patrol the elongated law courts along the Grand Canal. Designed in 1552–5 by Sansovino, the courts are recognizable by their 25 plain arcades.

10 Grand Canal Views

The Erberia, right on the Grand Canal, makes a wonderful spot for boat-watching. Alternatively, wander on to the Rialto Bridge for a different vantage point.

RIALTO MARKET

Rialto market's narrow alleyways carry names such as Orefici (goldsmiths), Pescaria (fishmongers) and Erberia (vegetables), because the same type of shops once stood together. Local restaurants for market traders also had evocative names such as Scimia (Monkey) and Do Mori (Two Moors).

TORCELLO

H1

Reached by a beautiful 60-minute ferry ride from northern Venice, the laid-back island of Torcello is home to the oldest building on the lagoon – the basilica. The island was first settled in the 5th century by mainlanders fleeing invading Lombards and Huns. Sadly, few clues to this intriguing past survived once the power base shifted to Venice. Today, Torcello's green fields, tranquil canals and pastel-hued houses offer a welcome escape from the bustling streets of the city.

1 Torcello Basilica Exterior

Torcello 30142 041 730 119 Hours vary, call ahead

A miraculous survivor, this striking cathedral was founded in 639, and is the lagoon's oldest building. It was radically modified in 1008 but retains its Romanesque form, brick walls and its arcaded 9th-century portico.

2 Paving, Basilica

In vivid swirls of colours, rivalling the flooring in Basilica San Marco (p22), are brilliant 11th-century tesserae of stone and glass. Cubes, semicircles and triangles are laid into square designs. The floor level was raised 30 cm (12 inches) during the basilica's reconstruction.

3 Doomsday Mosaics, Basilica

In these superb mosaics dating from the 12th and 13th centuries, *The Last Judgment* is dramatically depicted in carefully restored scenes of devils, wild beasts and fires.

4 Apse Mosaics, Basilica

The Virgin, in a blue robe with gold fringing, is depicted cradling her radiant child in this moving 13th-century mosaic. Below her are the 12 apostles standing in a meadow of flowers.

5 Iconostasis, Basilica

Rich marble panels dating from 1100 show

Tranquil setting of the Torcello Basilica

peacocks drinking at the fountain of eternal life and, small lions posing under a tree full of birds. Alongside, six columns support 15th-century paintings of the apostles with the Virgin.

The 19th-century Museo dell'Estuario

6 Campanile

☐ Torcello Basilica ☐ Mar–Oct: 10:30am–5:30pm daily; Nov–Feb: 10am–5pm daily ⏎

The views from this simple 55-m (180-ft) bell tower reach over the vast expanse of the lagoon, with its meandering canals and tidal flats, to the Adriatic Sea, Venice itself and even north to the Alps on a clear winter's day.

7 Throne of Attila

By popular belief this marble armchair was the throne of the king of the Huns, though historical sources claim it was for the island's magistrates.

8 Museo dell'Estuario

☐ Torcello 30175 ☐ 041 730 761 ☐ Hours vary, call ahead ⏎

An intriguing, if modest, collection of archaeological finds from the island and treasures from the church are housed in the adjoining Gothic buildings.

9 Locanda Cipriani

A favourite of Ernest Hemingway, who stayed here (p150) in 1948, this guesthouse has a quiet charm that has attracted many celebrities since it opened in 1938. Diana, Princess of Wales, and actress Kim Novak are among them. Extend your stay in Torcello by spending a night here.

10 Santa Fosca

Alongside the basilica is this elegant church based on the design of a Greek cross. It's encircled by a five-sided colonnaded portico and houses St Fosca's tomb. Greek marble columns and carved capitals add to its beauty. The inside of the church is closed to visitors during services.

ATTILA THE HUN

The "Scourge of God", or the King of the Huns, ruled from 434 to 453 CE over an empire that stretched from the Alps and the Baltic towards the Caspian Sea. As part of his campaign against the Roman Empire, Attila attacked Milan, Verona and Padua, and refugees fled to Torcello. Burning the cathedral town of Aquileia gave him great satisfaction – his men raised a hill in Udine so he could enjoy the sight.

Elegant red-brick church of Santa Fosca

TOP TIP

Stop by the stone "Devil's Bridge", near the Locanda Cipriani, to snap a photo.

CAMPO SANTA MARGHERITA

📍 K5

This cheery, picturesque square in the district of Dorsoduro is a hive of activity day in, day out. It owes its name to the Christian martyr St Margaret of Antioch, possibly a fictitious figure, but highly popular in medieval times. Lined with houses from the 14th and 15th centuries, Campo Santa Margherita consists of market stalls, offbeat shops and cafés, creating a lively hub that attracts a young crowd.

1 Palazzo Foscolo-Corner

This beautiful palace is virtually unchanged since the 1300s and instantly distinguishable by its sizable overhanging eaves. A striking Byzantine-style lunette, bearing an inset with the family crest, tops the entrance portal.

2 Ex Chiesa di Santa Margherita

This deconsecrated church has been restored by the University of Venice, and is now the Auditorium Santa Margherita. A writhing 14th-century dragon symbolizing the martyrdom of St Margaret enlivens the foot of the bell tower.

3 Calle del Forno

An unusual series of medieval-style projections from a first-floor dwelling, partly held up by brick columns, is one of the most interesting features of this busy thoroughfare leading to Piazzale Roma and the bus terminal. The street is named after a long-gone *forno* (bakery).

> 🍽 **EAT**
> Head to the local cafés and bars for a budget lunch – grab a pizza, *tramezzini* (sandwiches) or panini (rolls).

The Capitol Room, Scuola Grande dei Carmini

4 Scuola Grande dei Carmini

🅐 Dorsoduro 2617
🕙 10am–5pm daily
🌐 scuolagrandecar mini.it 📷

Glorious rooms adorned with Tiepolo's master-pieces, are highlights of this confraternity. The upstairs ceiling shows *St Simon Stock Receiving the Scapular from the Virgin*.

5 Scuola dei Varoteri

A splendid bas-relief of the Virgin sheltering a group of tradesmen in adoration graces the former tanners' guild dating from 1725.

Because of its isolated position, it was once mistakenly thought to be the house of the city's executioner.

6 The "House of the Moor"

Shakespeare's *Othello* was based on Cristoforo Moro, who was sent to govern Cyprus from 1508. This house at No. 2615 is his former home.

7 Corte del Fondaco

A charming covered passageway leads through to this minor courtyard where curious, low, bricked-in arches indicate the former site of a 1700s flour store. The name *fondaco* – or store – is derived from the Arabic word *fonduq*.

8 Chiesa di Santa Maria dei Carmini

This church survived Napoleon's suppression of the Carmelite order of monks in the adjoining monastery. Many of its 13th-century features are intact, such as the sculpted entrance porch.

9 Altana Terraces

These timber roof platforms were common

Campo Santa Margherita, dominated by its bell tower

A charming altana terrace in the square

in Venetian palaces, used by women for bleaching their hair in the sun. They are now used for laundry and partying on summer evenings, and can be seen around Campo Santa Margherita.

10 Rio Nuovo

Excavated in 1932–3 to form a short-cut from Piazzale Roma to the Grand Canal, the canal has been closed to vaporetti since the 1990s, due to building damage.

PEGGY GUGGENHEIM COLLECTION

📍 D5 🏛 Fondamenta Venier dei Leoni, Dorsoduro 704 (2nd entrance Calle S Cristoforo, Dorsoduro 701) ⏰ 10am–6pm Wed–Mon (last adm: 5pm) 🚫 25 Dec 🌐 guggenheim-venice.it 📷

The Peggy Guggenheim Collection is home to works by over 200 avant-garde artists. Put together by its far-sighted namesake, this is one of Dorsoduro's most visited sights. The complex (Peggy Guggenheim's former home), includes a striking sculpture garden.

1 Magic Garden
This deliberately child-like piece (1926) by Paul Klee (1879–1940) demonstrates the artist's abstract style. The work features blurry shapes and sketched-in faces and buildings.

2 Maiastra
A geometric masterpiece by Romanian artist Constantin Brancusi (1876–1957), this polished brass sculpture (1912) represents the magical bird who accompanies and protects the hero of Romanian fairy tales.

3 The Poet
Dating from the early Cubist period of legendary Spanish artist

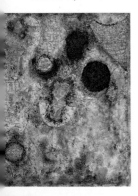

Magic Garden by Paul Klee

📷 **VIEW**
Don't miss the stunning panoramic views of Dorsoduro and the Grand Canal from the terrace of the museum.

Pablo Picasso (1881–1973), this portrait (1911) reimagines the human form. The figure is executed from a limited palette of ochre and dark browns.

4 Empire of Light
René Magritte's (1898–1967) clever use of light in this paradoxical combination of day and

Palazzo Venier dei Leoni, the home of the collection

night (1953–4) is noteworthy. Darkened trees and a house silhouetted by a street lamp are contrasted with a daytime sky with fluffy clouds in this work. The Belgian Surrealist was renowned for his eccentric subjects.

5 The Antipope

This unforgettable portrayal (1940) of a grotesque orange-robed bride assisted by mutant animals and humans (below) is by German Surrealist artist Max Ernst (1891–1976). Ernst was married to Peggy Guggenheim from 1942 to 1946, and the canvas is influenced in part by their tumultuous relationship.

6 The Moon Woman

This vibrant canvas (1942) starring a skeletal stick figure with an odd, padded curve is

an early work by Jackson Pollock (1912–56), pre-dating his famous "drip" technique.

7 Angel of the City

Set on steps leading to the terrace, this bronze horse and rider (1948) by Italian sculptor Marino Marini (1901–80) greet passing boats. It is one of the collection's most provocative pieces

8 Three Standing Figures

Beautifully placed in the Nasher Sculpture Garden, these bronze sculptures (1953) by Henry Moore (1898–1986) were inspired by Italian bell towers and African sculpture.

9 Mobile

This simple masterpiece of movement (1941) by American sculptor Alexander Calder (1898–1976), which gave its name to all mobiles, hangs in the atrium of Guggenheim's house.

10 Woman Walking

A serene elongated form of a truncated female figure, dating from 1932 and apparently inspired by Etruscan design, this sculpture is the recognizable trademark of the Swiss artist Alberto Giacometti (1901–66). He was a short-term participant in the Surrealist movement.

Peggy Guggenheim Collection Floorplan

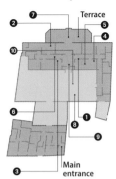

Key
- ■ Gallery
- ■ Nasher Sculpture Garden

PEGGY GUGGENHEIM

This heir to a mining fortune (1898–1979) first came to Europe in 1921, and quickly settled into Bohemian Paris. Resolving to "buy a picture a day", she amassed a contemporary art collection before she made Venice her home in 1947. She is fondly remembered by locals for her faithful dogs and for owning the city's last private gondola.

TOP 10 OF EVERYTHING

Venetian Carnival masks

PALACES

1 Ca' d'Oro
The original lapis lazuli, vermilion and gold façade has long faded, but the Gothic delicacy of this "golden palace" (p108) is intact, with marble tracery and arcaded loggias.

2 Doge's Palace
The Doge's Palace (p28) was the powerhouse of the city's rulers for nearly 900 years. Passing through the maze of gilded rooms gives an insight into its extravagance; the walls of the Sala dello Scudo, once part of the doge's private apartments, are covered with maps of the world. It's not all absolute luxury, though; the building also featured a torture chamber.

3 Ca' Foscari
⊞ L5 ⬥ **Calle Foscari, Dorsoduro 3246** ⬥ **For pre-booked guided tours only** ⬥ **unive.it** ⬥
Set on a strategic bend of the Grand Canal, Ca' Foscari has a series of mullioned windows facing the water, surmounted by an Istrian stone frieze. Once home to Doge Francesco Foscari, it is part of the University of Venice today.

4 Palazzo Vendramin-Calergi
⊞ D2
This Renaissance residence, built by Italian architects Pietro Lombardo and Mauro Coducci, was home to a string of noble families including the Cretan merchant Calergi in 1589. Another famed tenant was composer Richard Wagner, who spent his final years here. The palace is now home to the glittering City Casino and the Wagner Museum.

5 Ca' Dario
⊞ D5 ⬥ **Campiello Barbaro** ⬥ **To the public**
Embellished with multicoloured round stones, (tondi) this privately owned, asymmetrical palace dates from 1486. It was built for Giovanni Dario, who was an ambassador to Constantinople. Dario negotiated a peace treaty here that brought long-term hostilities between Venice and the Turks to a temporary halt.

6 Palazzo Barbaro
⊞ M6 ⬥ **Rio dell'Orso, S Marco 2840** ⬥ **To the public**
Cole Porter, Sergei Diaghilev and Claude Monet are just a few former

Gothic-style façade of Ca' d'Oro overlooking the Grand Canal

guests of this private palazzo, which comprises two palaces, one of which was bought in the 19th century by the Curtis family of Boston. Henry James *(p59)* wrote *The Aspern Papers* here and used it as the setting for *The Wings of a Dove*.

7 Palazzo Mastelli

◪ D1 ◪ Rio della Madonna dell'Orto, Cannaregio 3932 ◪ To the public

This eclectic palazzo, on a peaceful back canal of Cannaregio, was the abode of three merchant brothers who came from the Morea (the Peloponnese) in 1112. The brothers' stone figures adorn the neighbouring Campo dei Mori *(p108)*. Lions, birds and a prominent camel can be seen on the palazzo's Gothic façade.

8 Palazzi Contarini degli Scrigni e Corfu

◪ B5 ◪ Calle Contarini Corfu, Dorsoduro 1057 ◪ To the public

A 15th-century residence, enlarged by architect Vincenzo Scamozzi for the 17th-century proprietor Contarini Scrigni ("of the coffers"), so-called for the vast wealth of his family. The rooftop "folly" served as a useful observatory for astronomers.

9 Palazzo Pisani-Moretta

◪ M4 ◪ Ramo Pisani e Barbarigo, S Polo 2766 ◪ To the public

This palazzo is the venue of a fabulous masked ball during Carnival, when VIP guests glide up in gondolas to the candlelit Gothic façade on the Grand Canal. Painters Tiepolo and Guarana contributed to the interior Baroque decorations.

10 Ca' Rezzonico

◪ L5 ◪ Fondamenta Rezzonico, Dorsoduro 3136 ◪ Nov–Mar: 10am–5pm daily (last adm: an hour before closing) ◪ visitmuve.it ◪

This palace adorned with Tiepolo ceiling frescoes, Murano glass chandeliers and beautiful period furniture is now home to the museum of 18th-century Venice.

TOP 10
ARCHITECTURAL FEATURES OF A PALAZZO

Typical palazzo on the Grand Canal

1. Canal Entrance
This is where the family's private gondolas were moored and visitors were received.

2. Piano Nobile
The high-ceilinged first floor of a palazzo hosts the sumptuous salons and family's living quarters.

3. Façade
Usually fronting a canal, this was the only exterior wall decorated with a costly stone overlay to impress visitors.

4. Funnel-Shaped Chimneys
These and many other variations punctuate rooftops, their long shafts often running along outside walls.

5. Kitchen
This was always located on the ground floor for practical reasons.

6. Central Well
The well received filtered rain water for the palazzo's main water supply.

7. Entrance Portal
The importance of the main entrance was usually indicated by the distinctive family crest.

8. Enclosed Courtyard
This bustling area, usually with store rooms, was often used for the family's business transactions.

9. Altana Roof Terrace-Platform
These open-air areas were traditionally used for hanging out the washing or bleaching hair in the sun.

10. Land Access
Private gondolas rendered this relatively unimportant and hence, a narrow alley sufficed in its stead.

CHURCHES

1 Basilica di San Marco
Venice's famous landmark, this basilica *(p22)* dominates the east side of Piazza San Marco. It blends the architectural and decorative styles of East and West. The interior is embellished with golden mosaics, icons and ornate marble carvings.

2 Santa Maria Gloriosa dei Frari
Behind the brick façade of this Gothic church *(p40)* is an airy interior featuring grandiose works of art. These include Giovanni Bellini's *Madonna and Child*, Titian's famous *Assumption of the Virgin* and Donatello's wooden statue of John the Baptist.

3 Santi Giovanni e Paolo
🅥 E3 🅐 Campo SS Giovanni e Paolo, Castello 🕒 9am–6pm Mon–Sat, noon–6pm Sun 🆆 santigiovanniepaolo.it 🎟
The tombs of 25 doges are housed in this church built by Dominican friars from the 13th to 15th centuries. Among them is the tribute to Pietro Mocenigo for his valorous struggle to defend Venice's eastern colonies against the Turks (west wall). Inside are works of art including paintings by Veronese and a polyptych (1465) by Giovanni Bellini.

4 Santa Maria dei Miracoli
A favourite church *(p107)* among Venetians for weddings, Pietro

Santa Maria dei Miracoli's exquisite barrel-vaulted ceiling

The Santa Maria della Salute with gondolas in the foreground

Lombardo's masterpiece (1481–9) is resplendent again after restoration to deal with rising damp. The problem is not new – in Renaissance times marble slabs were affixed to the brick exterior with a cavity left for air flow. The ceiling gleams with gilt miniatures of holy figures.

5 Santa Maria della Salute
🅥 D5 🅐 Campo della Salute, Dorsoduro 🕒 9am–noon & 3–5:30pm daily 🎟
This great Baroque church dominates the southernmost entrance to the Grand Canal. Its silhouette has become one of Venice's most well-known landmarks. Designed by architect Longhena in 1630, it has a spacious interior and the altar houses a precious Byzantine icon. Dramatic works by Titian and Tintoretto can be seen in the sacristy.

6 San Giorgio Maggiore
Andrea Palladio's harmoniously proportioned 16th-century church *(p126)*, inspired by Greek temple design, stands across the water from Piazza San Marco. The interior is offset by two dynamic paintings by Tintoretto from

1594, *The Last Supper* and *Gathering the Manna*, on the chancel walls. The bell tower offers scenic views over Venice. Don't miss the monks' Gregorian chants every Sunday at 11am.

7 San Zaccaria
F4 ☐ Campo S Zaccaria, Castello ☐ 10am–noon & 4–6pm Mon–Sat, 4–6pm Sun & public hols ☐ Chapels & crypt

An intricate 15th-century façade by Coducci and, inside, Giovanni Bellini's superb *Madonna and Saints* (1505) are highlights of this church. The adjoining convent, now a police station, used to host puppet shows to entertain the nuns.

8 Chiesa di San Sebastiano
Renaissance painter Paolo Veronese (1528–88) spent a large part of his life joyously decorating the ceiling, walls, organ doors and altar of this unassuming 16th-century church (*p102*). He was buried among his masterpieces.

9 Madonna dell'Orto
D1 ☐ Campo Madonna dell'Orto, Cannaregio ☐ 10am–5pm Mon–Sat, noon–5pm Sun ☐ events.veneziaunica.it ☐

Eleven huge canvases by devout parishioner Tintoretto enhance this graceful Gothic church. Two masterpieces flank the high altar – the gruesome *The Last Judgment* and the soaring grandeur of *The Making of the Golden Calf*, both thought to have been painted around 1563.

10 San Pantalon
K4 ☐ Campo S Pantalon, Dorsoduro ☐ 10am–12:30pm & 3:30–6pm Mon–Thu, 10am–noon & 3:30–7pm Sat, 9am–12:30pm & 3:30–6pm Sun ☐ sanpantalon.it

Two treasures lurk behind a ramshackle façade: a nail from the True Cross and an incredible ceiling (1680–1704) by Gian Antonio Fumiani, a labour of love that ended when he purportedly plunged to his death.

TOP 10 SHRINES AND TABERNACLES

1. St Anthony
☐ D2 ☐ Calle Larga, Cannaregio
This 1668 "wardrobe" is full of fresh flower offerings.

2. Sottoportego de la Madonna
☐ D3 ☐ Sant' Aponal, S Polo
Pope Alexander III took refuge here from Emperor Barbarossa in 1177.

3. Gondolier's Shrine
☐ R5 ☐ Ponte della Paglia, S Marco
A 1583 Madonna shrine greets boats approaching the bridge.

4. Corte Nova
☐ G4 ☐ Castello
There are painted images over a lace-trimmed mantlepiece.

5. Covered Passageway
☐ F4 ☐ Calle Zorzi, Castello
The Virgin's protection has been implored here against plague and enemy attacks.

6. Scuola Grande della Misericordia
☐ D2 ☐ Cannaregio
Carvings of laden boats seek protection for the ferries, which set out from here.

7. Corte de Ca' Sarasina
☐ H5 ☐ Castello
This is a shrine dating back to the 1600s in memory of the dead.

8. Ponte del Fontego
☐ F3 ☐ Campo S Giustina, Castello
Each side of this Neo-Classical bridge features gondola bas-reliefs.

9. Gondola Traghetto Point
☐ L4 ☐ S Tomà, S Polo
There is a shrine to the Madonna, set on a pole, in the Grand Canal.

10. Boatmen's Pole
This tabernacle can be spotted midway on the San Giuliano–Venice channel.

FAMOUS VENETIANS

Queen Caterina Cornaro, the last monarch of Cyprus

1 Caterina Cornaro

This Venetian noblewoman (1454–1510) married the king of Cyprus, then allegedly poisoned him, thus securing the strategic island for Venice. Her return to the city was an occasion of great pomp, recalled to this day in a waterborne procession during the Regata Storica (p81). Cornaro's reward was the hilltown of Asolo.

2 Antonio Vivaldi

Vivaldi (1678–1741) was both an accomplished musician and an influential Baroque composer. Of his 500 concertos, *The Four Seasons* is the best known. J S Bach was a noted fan and transcribed ten of his concertos. Vivaldi spent extended periods of time teaching music at the Pietà home (p113) for girls.

3 Giacomo Casanova

This marvellous romantic figure (1725–98) was variously a diplomat, scholar, trainee priest, adventurer, gambler, notary's clerk, violinist, womanizer, exile, millionaire, writer and spy. He was imprisoned in the Doge's Palace (p28) on charges of being a magician, from where he effected an infamously daring escape.

4 Claudio Monteverdi

This late Renaissance madrigalist (1567–1643) is attributed with the introduction of the solo voice to theatre. His opera *Proserpina Rapita* was the first to be performed in Venice. After long periods at the court of the Gonzagas, he accepted an appointment at the Basilica di San Marco and worked for the Scuola Grande di San Rocco (p95).

5 John Cabot

Italian navigator Giovanni Caboto, or John Cabot (1450–99), and his sons were authorized by Henry VII of England to search for new lands with the aim of furthering trade. Believing himself to be on the north-east coast of Asia, he landed on Newfoundland in Canada and claimed it for England, opening up cod fishing.

6 Elena Lucrezia Corner Piscopia

It was inconceivable for the church in 1678 that a woman should teach religion, so the University of Padua awarded this child prodigy and the first female graduate (1646–84) a degree in philosophy, instead of one in theology to which she aspired.

7 Daniele Manin

Organizer of the 1848 rebellion against Austrian rule, this Venetian patriot (1804–57) is commemorated by a statue in Campo Manin. An independent "republic" was declared and survived 17 months of bombardments and even cholera, concluding with Manin's exile to Paris.

8 Paolo Sarpi

In 1509 when the Pope excommunicated Venice for insubordination, which involved restrictions on church construction and the refusal to hand over two priests on criminal charges, Sarpi (1552–1623) resolved the incident. A patriot and theologian, he was an advocate of division between State and Church.

9 Marco Polo

The legendary Cathay and the kingdom of the mighty Kublai Khan took pride of place in the explorer Marco Polo's best-selling account of his 20-year odyssey to the Far East, *Book of the Marvels of the World*. The son of a Venetian merchant, Polo (1254–1324) is responsible for the introduction of pasta and window blinds to the western world.

10 Luigi Nono

This musician (1924–90) made milestone progress in the field of electronic music, and an archive named after him was set up in Venice in 1993. A committed Communist, his works were often provocative. Nono's first opera *Intolleranza*, an attack on capitalism and colonialism, caused a riot at its premiere in 1961 in Venice.

Luigi Nono, an avant-garde composer of classical music

TOP 10
FOREIGN COMMUNITIES

Monet's painting *Le Grand Canal*

1. French
Painter Claude Monet and writers Théophile Gautier and Marcel Proust were drawn to Venice in the late 1800s.

2. Greeks
Here since 1498, the Greeks are the longest surviving group, still active with their own church.

3. Armenians
Fleeing Turkish invasion, in 1717 a close-knit religious group was granted an island by the Republic (p126).

4. Dalmatians *(Slavs)*
Traders from a historical region of Croatia, whose boats gave their name to the Riva degli Schiavoni (p112).

5. Turks
Although the Turks were enemies of Venice, the Republic still rented them a trade centre between 1621 and 1898.

6. Jewish
The Spanish Inquisition forced many Jewish people from other European countries to settle here.

7. Albanians
Calle degli Albanesi near Piazza San Marco is named in honour of this large 15th-century community.

8. Germans
The former German trade headquarters Fondaco dei Tedeschi attracted artists such as Albrecht Dürer.

9. British
Extended sojourns here were de rigueur for the British upper class during the 19th-century Grand Tour.

10. Americans
Leading literary figures and patrons of the arts have paid long-term visits since the 19th century.

WRITERS IN VENICE

1 Carlo Goldoni
"Italy's Molière" (1707–93) is celebrated at the Venetian theatre named in his honour *(p70)*. Performances of his lively, witty comedies are staged in Venetian dialect and feature recognizable local characters. The prolific playwright moved to Paris and was rewarded with a royal pension, but died destitute due to the French Revolution.

2 Thomas Mann
The sombre 1912 novel *Death in Venice* was both written and set in Venice and the Lido resort by this German Nobel Prize-winner (1875–1955). It tells the story of an ageing writer in dire need of relaxation who visits the city, but in the wake of an impossible infatuation slowly succumbs to the spreading cholera epidemic and dies.

3 William Shakespeare
Although he never visited Italy, let alone Venice, the English Bard (1564–1616) used accounts by contemporary travellers for the plots of *The Merchant of Venice* and *Othello*, portraying a city buzzing with trade and intrigue. *Romeo and Juliet* is set in nearby Verona *(p130)*.

4 Thomas Coryate
The very first traveller to write a detailed description of Venice in English, this eccentric gentleman from Somerset, England (1577–1617), compiled *Crudities, with Observations of Venice* (1611): "Such is the rarenesse of the situation of Venice, that it doth even amaze and drive into admiration all strangers that upon their first arrival behold the same."

5 Johann Wolfgang von Goethe
The story goes that this German literary giant (1749–1832) had his first ever view of the sea from Venice's Campanile. His first visit to the city and Italy was an experience of personal renewal. The account, published as *Italian Journey* (1786–8), is considered an early classic of travel literature.

6 Lord Byron
Eccentricities such as a menagerie of foxes and monkeys, not to mention swimming feats in the Grand Canal, made the English Romantic poet (1788–1824) something of a legend during his three-year sojourn here. His Venice-inspired work included *The Two Foscari* and the fourth canto of his autobiographical work *Childe Harold's Pilgrimage*.

7 John Ruskin
The meticulous, if opinionated, labour of love of this British art critic (1819–1900), *The Stones of Venice* was the first work to focus on the city's unique architectural heritage and Gothic style, as opposed to the art. The book was largely the outcome of a visit to the city in 1849.

A portrait of famous playwright William Shakespeare

American war correspondent and writer, Ernest Hemingway

8 Ernest Hemingway
This US Nobel Prize-winner (1899–1961) experienced Italy as a volunteer ambulance driver in World War I (recounted in *A Farewell to Arms*) and was wounded near Treviso. *Across the River and into the Trees* is set in Harry's Bar (*p35*).

9 Henry James
The leitmotif of this US novelist (1843–1916) was the contrast between what he saw as the spontaneity of the Americas and the staidness of Europe. Between 1872 and 1909 he compiled *Italian Hours*, a "travel diary", with plenty of comments on Venice.

10 Charles Dickens
The great English novelist (1812–70) spent a brief period in Venice during a tour of Italy, and the city inspired a dream sequence in his work *Pictures from Italy* (1846).

TOP 10
BACKGROUND READS

1. Acqua Alta, Donna Leon
From the best-selling mystery series featuring detective Guido Brunetti.

2. Venice, Jan Morris
An expert account of the delights of the city and its maritime history.

3. Venice, an Anthology Guide, Milton Grundy
A guide around town, seen through the eyes of famous writers.

4. Ruskin's Venice, editor Arnold Whittick
A very readable version of Ruskin's landmark work.

5. Stone Virgin, Barry Unsworth
A mystery involving the 15th-century statue of a famous courtesan.

6. Histoire de ma Vie, Giacomo Casanova
Autobiography detailing his famous escape (*p56*).

7. Dead Lagoon, Michael Dibdin
Detective Aurelio Zen navigates Venice's murky waters fraught with unease and intrigue.

8. The Architecture of Venice, Deborah Howard
An unbeatable architectural classic.

9. Stabat Mater, Tiziano Scarpa
Set in the Ospedale della Pietà, Venice's music school, at the beginning of the 18th century.

10. Death in Venice, Thomas Mann
A portrayal of desire and decadence amid the fog.

Donna Leon, author of *Acqua Alta*

ARTISTS IN VENICE

1 Jacopo Tintoretto
The great Mannerist of the late Renaissance, Tintoretto (1518–94) produced huge, glowing canvases, seen at his main showcase the Scuola Grande di San Rocco *(p95)*, as well as his parish church Madonna dell'Orto *(p55)*.

2 Titian (Tiziano Vecellio)
A native of the Cadore region, whose awe-inspiring Dolomite peaks often feature in his highly coloured dynamic compositions, Titian (1488–1576) came to Venice when young and studied under Giovanni Bellini.

3 Paolo Veronese
Foremost painter of the Venetian School, Veronese (1528–88) created huge canvases in classical settings and teeming with people. His works are on display in the Doge's Palace *(p26)* and the Chiesa di San Sebastiano *(p102)*.

4 Canaletto (Giovanni Antonio Canal)
Famous for his landscapes of Venice and England, Canaletto (1697–1768) thrived under the patronage of the British consul Joseph Smith. Unfortunately, very few of his paintings can be seen in Venice.

Giovanni Bellini's magnificently coloured *Madonna del Prato* (1505)

5 Giovanni Bellini
Giovanni Bellini (1430–1516), with his father Jacopo and brother Gentile, made Venice one of the greatest centres of Renaissance art. His anatomy studies added great precision to his work. His trademarks are radiant Madonnas, serene St Peters and brilliant satiny robes.

6 Marietta Robusti
Known as "la Tintoretta", Robusti (1554–1590) was the illegitimate daughter of Tintoretto and, dressed as a boy, followed her father to his

workshop. The only painting conclusively attributed to her is a self-portrait in the Uffizi Gallery in Florence. She is buried in Madonna dell'Orto (*p55*), where Tintoretto also lies.

7 Vittorio Carpaccio

This Renaissance master (1465–1525) delighted in remarkably detailed scenes of daily life in contemporary Venice. His original narrative style and marvellous command of light characterize his many narrative cycles on display at the Accademia galleries (*p38*) and the Scuola di San Giorgio degli Schiavoni (*p63*).

8 Giorgione

A native of Castelfranco Veneto, Giorgione (1477–1510) came to Venice when young to serve as an apprentice under Giovanni Bellini. In his brief life, he produced memorable mood works that he never signed. One of his most famous works, *The Tempest*, can be seen in the Accademia (*p38*).

9 Pietro Longhi

Longhi (1702–85) painted witty scenes of the everyday life of the well-to-do folk in Venice. Examples of his work can be admired at the Fondazione Querini Stampalia (*p62*), as well as in Ca' Rezzonico (*p53*). Many figures can be seen wearing the traditional Venetian mask.

10 Rosalba Carriera

A Venetian Rococo portraitist, Carriera (1673–1757) was the most appreciated miniaturist of her time, with her work adorning snuff boxes. Her subjects included mythological and allegorical figures as well as portraits from everyday life. She also pioneered the use of pastels.

Canaletto's stunning *View of the Grand Canal* (c 1735)

TOP 10 VENICE ARCHITECTS

1. Andrea Palladio (1508–80)
Regarded as one of the most influential architects of the western world, Palladio designed Classical villas in the Veneto and churches in Venice.

2. Jacopo Sansovino (1486–1570)
Outstanding architect who trained under – and took his name from – sculptor Andrea Sansovino. Examples of Jacopo's work are the Libreria (*p32*) and Zecca.

3. Baldassare Longhena (1598–1682)
Longhena's masterpiece, Santa Maria della Salute, was designed when he was just 26, but his flamboyant style is also seen in Ca' Rezzonico (*p53*).

4. Pietro Lombardo (1435–1515)
Lombardy native Pietro was director of works at the Doge's Palace. His trademark leafy bas-relief pattern is also seen at Santa Maria dei Miracoli (*p107*).

5. Mauro Coducci (c 1440–1504)
The Renaissance designs of Lombardy native Coducci can be seen in Palazzo Vendramin-Calergi (*p52*).

6. Bartolomeo Bon (1374–1464)
Sculptor and architect Bon's designs were the basis for the church and Scuola di San Rocco and the Ca' d'Oro (*p108*).

7. Michele Sanmicheli (1484–1559)
Original military fortification designs by this Mannerist architect are found in his home town of Verona.

8. Antonio Da Ponte (1512–95)
This engineer and architect is well known for the Rialto Bridge (*p95*).

9. Giannantonio Selva (1757–1819)
In Venice, Selva is best known for the elegant Fenice theatre (*p71*).

10. Carlo Scarpa (1906–78)
Modernist Scarpa reorganized both the Accademia and the Querini Stampalia along Japanese-inspired lines.

MUSEUMS AND GALLERIES

1 Accademia Galleries
The Accademia's *(p38)* collection of Venetian paintings includes masterpieces by Titian, Bellini and Giorgione. The real treasure is the *Miracle of the Cross at the Rialto* by Carpaccio, for its depiction of a Black gondolier. The Accademia isn't just for art lovers – it's a must for all.

2 Museo del Vetro
G2 Fondamenta Giustinian 8, Murano ◷10am–5pm daily (Apr–Oct: to 6pm; last adm: an hour before closing) ⓦvisitmuve.it ⚡
A phenomenal chandelier from 1864, constructed with 356 handmade pieces,

is the star of this glass museum in the Palazzo Giustiniani. Other exhibits include Phoenician phials, blown vases, ruby chalices, exquisite mirrors and the famed kaleidoscopic beads that were once traded worldwide.

3 Palazzo Grassi
This collection of contemporary art, housed in a palace *(p88)* on the Grand Canal, changes on a regular basis. The inspirational sister gallery is Punta della Dogana *(p102)*.

4 Fondazione Querini Stampalia
R4 Campo S Maria Formosa, Castello 5252 ◷10am–6pm Tue–Sun ⓦquerinistampalia.org ⚡
An unmissable Renaissance palace, this was the bequest of Giovanni Querini in 1868, the last member of the Querini dynasty, on the condition that the library be made available "particularly in the evenings for the convenience of scholars". The restored palace-museum houses scenes of public and private life by Gabriel Bella and Pietro Longhi, as well as Carlo Scarpa's Modernist creations.

Murano glassware at Museo del Vetro

Magnificent interior of the Museo Correr

5 Museo Correr

A tremendous number of priceless artworks and a miscellany of items on Venice's history are housed in this fine museum *(p32)* on Piazza San Marco.

6 Museo del Merletto

🔲 H1 🏠 Baldassare Galuppi 187, Burano 🕐 10am–4pm Tue–Sun (last adm: 3:30pm) 🌐 museomerletto. visitmuve.it

A must for craft-lovers, the island of Burano is home to the Museo del Merletto. It displays over 200 rare lace items, documenting a 500-year history.

7 Ca' Pesaro Galleria d'Arte Moderna

🔲 N1 🏠 Fondamenta Ca' Pesaro, S Croce 2076 🕐 10am–5pm Tue–Sun (Apr–Oct: to 6pm; last adm: an hour before closing) 🌐 capesaro. visitmuve.it

A Baroque triumph, Ca' Pesaro's interior, in contrast, houses works by European 19th- and 20th-century masters such as Marc Chagall and Gustav Klimt. There's also a strong collection of Italian works.

8 Scuola di San Giorgio degli Schiavoni

🔲 F4 🏠 Calle dei Furlani, Castello 3259 🕐 10am–5:30pm Wed–Mon 🌐 scuoladalmatavenezia.com

The finest works by Vittorio Carpaccio can be seen at the confraternity of the Slavs (Schiavoni). *Slaying The Dragon* is one of the scenes from the lives of Dalmatian saints, which were painted between 1502 and 1507.

9 Scuola Grande di San Rocco

The San Rocco *(p95)* confraternity has been turned into a gallery to display its spectacular collection of works by Tintoretto. The artist won the commission to decorate the walls and ceiling hands down – not content with a sketch, he completed an entire canvas. He then spent 23 years devoting himself to the cycle of 60 inspired Old and New Testament scenes, culminating in the breathtaking *Crucifixion* (1565). These masterpieces are the crowning glory of Tintoretto's life work.

10 Museo Storico Navale

🔲 G4 🏠 Campo S Biagio, Castello 2148 🕐 11am–6pm Wed–Mon 🌐 visitmuve.it

This historical naval museum has almost an entire floor dedicated to the history of the Venetian Republic's naval past. However, the highlight is the replica of the Doge's ceremonial barge, *Bucintoro*, decorated with allegorical statues. The museum also features the Ship Pavilion, a 2000 sq m (21,500 sq ft) extension, which displays ancient ceremonial gondolas, working lagoon boats and military ships.

The *Bucintora*, a replica of the Doge's barge, Museo Storico Navale

BRIDGES

1 Rialto Bridge
🔲 P3

Located at the narrowest point of the Grand Canal is Venice's most famous bridge *(p95)*. Its design was hotly contested: 16th-century architects Michelangelo, Sansovino and Palladio entered the competition, but lost out to Antonio da Ponte. There were two previous bridges on this site; a flimsy timber bridge that collapsed in 1444 under the weight of a crowd, then a drawbridge, which would be raised for the passage of tall-masted sailing ships.

2 Ponte della Libertà
🔲 A1

Truth and irony combine in the name of this 3.6-km (2-mile) "Bridge of Freedom": the first full link between the mainland and Venice was put in place in 1933, when Italy was living under Fascism. The construction was preceded 86 years earlier by the Austrian-built railway bridge across the lagoon. Before that, the city relied entirely on boats.

3 Ponte dei Tre Archi
🔲 B1

A favourite subject for artists, this unusual three-arched high bridge crosses the Cannaregio canal close to where it joins the lagoon. It dates from 1688 and was the work of engineer Andrea Tirali, nicknamed Tiranno ("the tyrant") by his employees.

4 Ponte degli Scalzi
🔲 J1

One of the city's most marvellous lookout points, over fascinating palaces and boats, can be found at the highest point of this elegant 40-m- (130-ft-) long bridge, which rises 7 m (23 ft) above the Grand Canal. Named after the nearby monastery of barefooted

Iconic Rialto Bridge linking the two sides of the Rialto

Rio Novo canal near Piazzale Roma. The timber and stone structures afford views of 13 other bridges.

9 Ponte della Costituzione
🗺 B3

Also known as the Ponte di Calatrava, named so after its designer Santiago Calatrava, this fourth bridge over the Grand Canal is modelled on a gondola's hull. It has attracted criticism since its 2008 inauguration due to its minimalist modern design and high cost of construction.

10 Bridge of Sighs
🗺 R5

This evocatively named bridge (p27) (known as Ponte dei Sospiri in Italian) once led convicts from the beautiful Doge's Palace (p26) to the horrors of the adjacent prisons. According to legend, the Bridge of Sighs takes its name from the lamentations of the prisoners as they made their way over to the offices of the feared State Inquisitors.

monks, this 1934 structure in Istrian stone by Eugenio Miozzi replaced an Austrian-built iron bridge.

5 Bridge with No Parapet
🗺 D2

One of only two remaining bridges with no side protection, this one spans a quiet side canal in Cannaregio. The other is the Ponte del Diavolo on Torcello.

6 Ponte dei Pugni
🗺 K5

Pugni (fistfights) between rival clans took place here until 1705 when they were outlawed for their violence. Stone footprints on the "Bridge of Fists" marked the starting point of the combat, but the contestants usually ended up throwing each other in the canal.

7 Ponte delle Tette
🗺 M2

When an increase in the practice of sodomy was recorded in the 1400s, the city's prostitutes were encouraged to display their feminine wares at the windows over the "Bridge of Breasts".

8 Tre Ponti
🗺 B3

This is not three ("tre") but five interlocking bridges spanning the

Gondolas passing below the Bridge of Sighs

OFF THE BEATEN TRACK

1 Pinacoteca Manfrediniana
📍 E6 🏛 Dorsoduro 1 🕐 10am–1pm & 3–5pm Thu & Fri, 10am–6pm Sat 🌐 manfrediana.it ♿

This museum owes its name to the marquis Federico Manfredini, whose paintings and prints were donated to Venice. The displays here include works by Bellini, Cima da Conegliano, Lippi and Vivarini.

2 Rio Terrà Rampani
📍 M2 🏛 San Polo

Just around the corner from Ponte delle Tette (p65) is this quiet thoroughfare. Referred to as the "Carampane" (Ca' Rampani), it was where sex workers were based in the Venetian Republic. The city had some 11,600 officially registered courtesans in the 1500s.

3 Corte del Duca Sforza
📍 L6 🏛 San Marco

This picturesque courtyard, which opens on to the Grand Canal, is surprisingly well hidden. It takes its name from the Duke of Milan who took over a partially constructed palace here in 1461, though work went no further than the diamond-point ashlar on the façade. The artist Titian used the building as a studio while he was working on the Doge's Palace (p26).

4 Celestia to Bacini Walkway
📍 G3 🏛 Castello

This unusual walkway clings to a perimeter wall of the ancient Arsenale shipyard in a rather neglected zone of Castello. It makes for an atmospheric walk, offering marvellous views over the lagoon and leading to a cluster of old workers' dwellings.

5 Corte dell'Anatomia
📍 L2 🏛 S Croce

This peaceful courtyard was named after the anatomy theatre that existed here in 1368. Much later, in 1671, in neighbouring Campo San Giacomo dall'Orio, a College of Anatomy was established in what is now a separate building. Today it has an attractive trellis draped with vines.

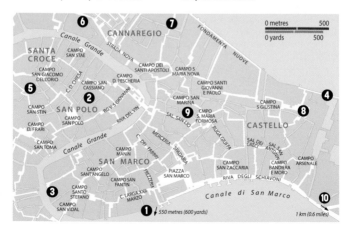

Typical 16th-century buildings in Campo della Maddalena

6 Campo della Maddalena
🗺 D2 🏠 Cannaregio

Just off the main thoroughfare Strada Nova is this beautiful raised square. It is often used as a film location, due to the fact that it has remained all but unchanged since medieval times. Its modest houses are topped with a fascinating range of chimneys.

7 Campo dei Gesuiti
🗺 E2 🏠 Cannaregio

A favourite spot for children to play, this is a spacious neighbourhood square. In addition to the Gesuiti (Jesuit) church, it is flanked by the cavernous Crociferi complex, erstwhile monastery, then barracks, now student lodgings. Wander inside to admire the cloisters and the canalside café.

8 Campo della Celestia
🗺 G3 🏠 Castello

Now a tranquil residential spot, back in the 1200s this square saw plenty of comings and goings due to the riotous behaviour of the sisters in the Cistercian convent. The first archive of city affairs was established here under Napoleon.

9 Calle del Paradiso
🗺 R3 🏠 Castello, San Lio

This attractive alley just off the busy San Lio thoroughfare is lined with medieval-style overhangs, as well as restaurants and shops. The name comes from the delightfully lopsided 15th-century arch, which depicts the Virgin and her devotees at the end of the alley.

10 Sant'Elena
🗺 H6

Located in the far eastern extremity of Venice, this quiet residential islet has marvellous shady parkland on the waterfront. Children can enjoy the skating rink and playground while parents relax in laidback cafés.

The islet of Sant'Elena, a green oasis in Castello

FAMILY ATTRACTIONS

1 Play Areas
Children tired of art and architecture can release their energy in the city's well-equipped playgrounds. Find slides, swings and frames at Parco Savorgnan near Ponte delle Guglie in Cannaregio and a fenced-in water-front park at Giardini in Castello (p114). The vast shady green expanse of Sant'Elena is another popular public park, and it even has a modest skating rink and an artificial climbing wall.

2 Ferry Trips
Restful for adults, exciting for youngsters, the varied boat lines

are an ideal way for families to appreciate the joys of the city. Get older children to plan trips on the route maps, but avoid the outside seating on the vaporetto with toddlers. For an extended trip, take the majestic double-decker *motonave* over to Lido and Punta Sabbioni (p121).

3 Peggy Guggenheim Collection
Every Sunday this museum (p48) hosts Art4Family, free educational workshops in English and Italian. The classes are run by artists and students from the Venice Academy of Fine Arts, and are aimed at children aged four to ten and their parents. Book in advance.

4 Museo di Storia Naturale
🗺 L1 🏛 Salizzada del Fondaco dei Turchi, S Croce 1730 🕐 9am–5pm daily (Jun–Sep: to 6pm; last adm: an hour before closing) 🌐 visitmuve.it 🔗

Housed in a palazzo on the Grand Canal, this museum covers over 700 million years of history withits two million-plus objects. The collection is organized into three sections: paleotology, exploration and nature.

A basketball court in Sant'Elena's public park

The highlight is a 3.6-m- (12-ft-) tall, 7-m- (23-ft-) long skeleton of the dinosaur *Ouranosaurus nigeriensis*.

5 Glassmaking Demonstrations

A great time is guaranteed at a glassblowing workshop. Small workshops are dotted all over Venice, while Murano *(p121)* has some large-scale furnaces. Demonstrations, which might include glass blown into a fine vase or myriad animal shapes, are free, on the condition that you stroll through the showroom afterwards.

6 Visiting the Lido

If younger children are starting to tire of the galleries and museums, take them to the fun-loving Lido *(p125)*. The free beaches offer hours of fun and not just in the summer. Bikes can also be hired.

7 Museo Storico Navale

Easily the best city museum *(p63)* for children, this three-floor

Sunseekers relaxing at one of the Lido's sandy beaches

Ships on display at the Museo Storico Navale

haven of shipbuilding includes Chinese junks and exhibits from World War II, such as the famed torpedoes guided by Italian Navy divers, responsible for sinking British warships. Divided into the history of the Venetian navy, the Italian navy from 1860 to today and a Swedish room, the layout and displays are excellent and there are informative explanations in English.

8 Ca' Macana

📍 K6 🏠 Calle delle Botteghe, Dorsoduro 3172 🌐 camacana.com

This mask shop offers short courses that are both fun and stimulating. Experienced instructors share their craft by explaining the time-honoured techniques of the Venetian mask-making tradition. Participants can choose from over 60 styles to make masks.

9 Doge's Palace Prisons and Armoury

Children are thrilled by the spooky labyrinth of narrow passageways through the palace's *(p26)* erstwhile prisons. Decipher the graffiti scratched on the walls by inmates over the centuries, and hunt for the unusual miniature suit from the 16th century, and armoured protection for horses in the armoury.

10 Mistero e Magia

📍 R4 🏠 Ruga Giuffa, Castello 4925 🕐 Sun

Run by a real magician, this shop is full of essentials such as wands, hats, and books revealing the tricks of the trade in Italian and English.

ENTERTAINMENT VENUES

Exterior of the iconic Teatro Goldoni on San Marco

summer the local cinemas screen some of the highlights from the Venice Film Festival.

1 Teatro Goldoni

📍 P4 🏠 Calle del Teatro, S Marco 4650/B 🌐 teatrostabileveneto.it

Teatro Goldoni is one of the oldest theatres in the city, dating from the 17th century. It acquired its present name in 1875 in honour of the 18th-century playwright Carlo Goldoni *(p58)*. An excellent range of international plays is performed in Italian between November and May.

2 Teatro Malibran

📍 Q2 🏠 Corte del Teatro Malibran, Cannaregio

In a quiet square near Rialto *(p42)* stands the Malibran Theatre, which was re-inaugurated in 2001 to take on part of the Fenice's productions. Dating back to 1678 as Teatro Grimani, it was renamed after the 19th-century Spanish mezzo-soprano Maria Malibran.

3 Films in English

📍 N4 🏠 Salizzada de la Chiesa o del Teatro 3997 🌐 comune.venezia.it/it/content/multisala-rossini

The Multisala Rossini is a three-screen cinema that shows selected films in English, including new releases. In late

4 Palazzo Barbarigo Minotto

📍 D5 🏠 Fondamenta Duodo o Barbarigo, San Marco 2504 🌐 musicapalazzo.com

A great way to experience grand operas, Musica a Palazzo performs each act of an opera in a different hall of the grand Palazzo Barbarigo Minotto. The travelling opera is a revival of a tradition that began at the end of the 19th century.

5 Vivaldi Concerts

📍 F4 🏠 Chiesa della Pietà, Riva degli Schiavoni, Castello 🌐 chiesavivaldi.it

Performances of Vivaldi's *Four Seasons* by I Virtuosi Italiani can be enjoyed in the church where it was composed. Designed by Giorgio Massari with the guidance of Vivaldi himself, the remarkable acoustics and frescoes by Tiepolo make for an inspiring experience.

6 Chamber Music

📍 M6 🏠 Chiesa di San Vidal, Campo S Vidal 🌐 interpreti veneziani.com

While listening to the uplifting notes of Vivaldi's *Four Seasons* or a masterpiece from Bach, this is the perfect spot to take a moment to unwind and relax from the day's hectic sightseeing. The Church of San Vidal was rebuilt around 1700 and has a spacious interior.

7 Concerts in Costume

📍 J5 🏠 Scuola Grande dei Carmini, Campo S Margherita, Dorsoduro 🌐 musicainmaschera.com

Talented young singers and musicians perform comic operas at the Scuola Grande dei Carmini *(p47)*. It makes for a memorable evening.

8 Palazzetto Bru Zane

L2 **S Polo 2368**
bru-zane.com

Housed in the ornate 17th-century Palazzetto Bru Zane, the Centre for French Romantic Music hosts concerts of French chamber music and symphonic and choral works dating between 1780 and 1920. It also organizes lectures, conferences and educational events. In addition, it offers the *Romantici in erba* programme, which includes outreach activities aimed at young audiences.

9 Auditorium Santa Margherita

K5 **Campo S Margherita, Dorsoduro 3689**

This converted church *(p46)* from the 9th century sometimes hosts world and other music performances for free. Details are generally posted on the door or online *(unive.it)*. It is located in one the liveliest areas in the city, easily reached from Piazzale Roma and the train station.

10 Teatro La Fenice

A glorious theatre *(p87)* and landmark in the history of opera and Italian theatre, Teatro La Fenice hosts world-famous opera and concert performances. It was re-inaugurated in December 2003. Productions range from Verdi and Rossini to contemporary composers. Buy tickets from Venezia Unica offices at the theatre or online.

Actors in costume at the famous Teatro La Fenice theatre and opera house

TOP 10 FILMS SET IN VENICE

Scene from *The Merchant of Venice*

1. Senso (1954)
Alida Valli betrays family and country for an Austrian officer in this Visconti film.

2. Anonimo Veneziano (1970)
This drama, directed by Enrico Maria Salerno, tells the story of a musician who dreams of becoming a conductor.

3. Death in Venice (1971)
Visconti's film starring Dirk Bogarde is now as classic as the Thomas Mann *(p59)* novel on which it is based.

4. Fellini's Casanova (1976)
Donald Sutherland walks around a fantasized version of Venice in this Fellini film.

5. The Wings of the Dove (1997)
Helena Bonham Carter stars in the film version of Henry James's Venetian story.

6. Indiana Jones and the Last Crusade (1989)
The church of San Barnaba serves as the setting for a Venetian library in this film.

7. Pane e Tulipan (2000)
Soldini's romantic comedy, "Bread and Tulips", follows a woman who hitchhikes to Venice.

8. The Merchant of Venice (2004)
An adaptation of Shakespeare's work starring Al Pacino as a brilliant Shylock.

9. Dieci Inverni (2009)
In this film by Valerio Mieli, two people fall in love over ten winters.

10. A Haunting in Venice (2023)
This supernatural crime-thriller, directed and interpreted by Kenneth Branagh, is loosely based on a novel by Agatha Christie.

CAFÉS AND OSTERIE (WINE BARS)

1 Un Mondo di Vino
⌖ E3 🏠 Salizzada S Canciano, Cannaregio 5984/A 🕐 Thu

Italian wines can be enjoyed at this converted butcher's shop, along with bar snacks such as *insalata di mare* (seafood salad) and regional cheeses. This place is well frequented by locals and visitors.

2 Osteria Ruga Rialto
⌖ N3 🏠 Ruga Vecchia S Giovanni, S Polo 692/A 🕐 Thu

Verging on rowdy, this traditional establishment turns out crisp fried calamari and vegetables at evening aperitivo time, when you'll have to elbow your way past the locals to reach the bar. Lunch and dinner are some-what quieter affairs.

3 Estro
⌖ K4 🏠 Calle San Pantalon, Dorsoduro 3778 🕐 Tue

Run by two Venetian brothers, this stylish *enoteca* serves a fantastic range of wines from all over the world, along with dishes made from locally grown, seasonal ingredients.

4 Osteria alla Frasca
⌖ E2 🏠 Corte della Carità, Cannaregio

Said to be the site where Titian kept his paints and canvases, this is now a tiny

picturesque bar serving drinks and snacks on a vine-covered terrace.

5 Cantine del Vino già Schiavi
⌖ C5 🏠 Fondamenta Nani, Dorsoduro 992 🕐 Sun

Join the locals at this family-run specialist wine cellar, located near the Accademia Bridge, for excellent prosecco at a stand-up bar. Simple nibbles to accompany the wine include mortadella sausage and panini filled with *sopressa*, a local salami.

6 Bar Filovia
⌖ B3 🏠 Fondamenta S Chiara 521, S Croce

Located under the Ponte della Costituzione, Bar Filovia is loved by locals for its wide selection of croissants and *tramezzini* (sandwiches). Classic fillings include mozzarella and tomato, but the house speciality is *piccantino* – prosciutto and spicy hot sauce.

7 Al Todaro
⌖ R5 🏠 Piazza S Marco 3, S Marco 🌐 al-todaro.it

This historic ice-cream parlour occupies a magical location in Piazza San Marco *(p30)*, overlooking the Grand Canal. The classic gelato flavours served here are reasonably priced.

Enjoying tasty gelato overlooking a Venetian waterway

8 Suso Gelatoteca

One of the most renowned *gelaterie* in Venice, Suso Gelatoteca *(p92)* has been serving its rich, homemade ice cream for years. It also offers vegan flavours, which are made with coconut milk and include a water-based dark chocolate scoop. Unlike other Venetian *gelaterie*, the gelato here is served in a crispy wafer cone – rather than a paper cup – so the entire thing is edible and hence, reduces waste.

9 Bar Spritz

📍 M5 🏠 Calle dei Frati 30, S Marco 3532/36 📞 328 595 09 07 🕒 Sun

A small bar with a few alfresco tables, ideal for enjoying a coffee and a croissant, a light lunch, or an aperitivo. The menu has everything from sweet pastries to savoury bruschetta, making it a great choice for breakfast, too. As an added bonus, the entire menu is excellent value for money.

10 Torrefazione Cannaregio

📍 C1 🏠 Fondamenta dei Ormesini, Cannaregio 2804 🌐 torrefazionecannaregio.it

Situated close to the Jewish Quarter *(p107)*, Torrefazione Cannaregio has walls stocked high with jars of different coffee beans. Pick from a variety of blends – from fruity flavours to 100 per cent Arabica – and enjoy a cup in the cafe's brick-and-dark-wood interior. Or, you can buy a paper bag of beans to take home with you. Tea and breakfast pastries are also on offer.

Alfresco seating at Al Todaro in Piazza San Marco

TOP 10 BEVERAGES

1. Spritz
Venetian favourite of white wine with a splash of Bitter, Aperol or Select (aperitivo brands) and a shot of mineral water.

2. Prosecco
Excellent dry white wine from the hills around Conegliano and Valdobbiadene.

3. Bellini
Smooth fresh peach juice and sparkling prosecco blend, invented by Cipriani of Harry's Bar *(p35)*.

4. Red Wine
Try a small glass of house wine *(ombra)* or a quality Cabernet, Valpolicella or Amarone.

5. White Wine
Soave and Pinot Grigio are worthwhile alternatives to house varieties.

6. Mineral Water
Widely consumed in Italy, either sparkling *(gasata)* or still *(naturale)*. Tap water is *acqua dal rubinetto*.

7. Fruit Drinks
These can be ordered as freshly squeezed juice *(spremuta)* or bottled nectars *(succo di frutta)*.

8. Coffee
Straight espresso, frothy cappuccino or caffè latte in a tall glass with hot milk can be found at cafés across the city.

9. Hot Chocolate
Usually served in the winter months. An espresso milk-free version can be found in good chocolate emporia.

10. Sgroppino
Made with lemon sorbet, vodka and prosecco, *sgroppino* is served between courses.

Aperol spritz at the Carnival

LOCAL DISHES

1 Frittelle Veneziane
Frittelle or *fritole* are fluffy Venetian fritters made from a soft dough flavoured with citrus peel, pine nuts and raisins, and sometimes filled with *zabaglione*, chocolate or Chantilly cream. They've been the official Carnival sweet since the Renaissance and can be found in pastry shops.

Frittelle, typically served during the Venice Carnival

2 Sarde in Saor
Sardines in vinegar is Venice's most emblematic and beloved dish. It honours the city's maritime past and consists of fried sardines layered in braised onions and dressed in pine nuts, raisins and bay leaves. The sardines are marinated for at least two days before being served cold.

3 Carpaccio
The most popular dish at Harry's Bar *(p35)*, beef carpaccio (traditionally made with sirloin) was invented by owner Giuseppe Cipriani in 1950 to satisfy Contessa Amalia Nani Mocenigo,

A beef carpaccio dish, best enjoyed at Harry's Bar

who adhered to a diet of raw meat. He called it "carpaccio" in honour of Venetian Renaissance painter Vittore Carpaccio who loved the colour red.

4 Antipasto Misti di Pesce
Almost every good Venetian restaurant offers a mixed fish platter showcasing lagoon special-ities. Platters typically feature sardines and prawns in vinegar (or *saor*), tiny grey shrimp *(schie)*, boiled baby octopus *(folpetti)*, a dollop of creamed cod *(baccala)*, and possibly some fish carpaccio (typically bream or swordfish) or spider crab.

5 Baccalà Mantecato
This famous Venetian dish dates to the era of the Republic when Venice was a global trading power and sailors brought home Norwegian salted cod. The dehydrated fish is soaked for several days before it's mashed with a mild virgin olive oil, creating a fluffy white creamy paste. It's served on crusty bread or slices of yellow polenta.

6 Risi e Bisi
You know spring has sprung in the lagoon when this Doge's dish of "rice and peas" appears on local menus. It consists of Veneto Vialone Nano rice which is cooked into a wet risotto with sweet Colognola ai Colli peas, giving it a vibrant green hue. Finally, it's finished with butter and parmesan, creating a deep, delicious flavour.

7 Purple Artichokes
The island of Sant'Erasmo is Venice's vegetable garden and its star is the small, local purple artichoke (carciofi violetti). At the start of the season (April–June) the first bud appears and is pruned to allow the other buds to grow better. These tender first buds are immediately shipped to restaurants where they are served sliced and raw in salads or simply dipped in olive oil.

8 Bigoli all'anatra
Bigoli comes from Venetian bigat meaning worm, which perfectly describes the appearance of this thick short pasta. Typically it's served with a rich duck (anatra) ragu.

9 Grilled Fish
Seabass (branzino), gilt-head bream (orata), mackerel (sgombro), mullet (triglia), flounder (passera) and John Dory (San Pietro) are just some of the fish found in the Venetian lagoon and likely to be served raw, simply grilled or lightly fried.

10 Spaghetti al Nero di Seppia
If you order this dish, you may be shocked by the jet black spaghetti that arrives at your table. That's thanks to the cuttlefish ink that is used to dye the freshly made spaghetti and the thick inky sauce that accompanies it – try it at Trattoria alla Madonna (p93). Beware, the ink (temporarily) stains your teeth.

Traditional Italian Spaghetti al Nero di Seppia

TOP 10 SPECIALITY LAGOON SEAFOOD

Spider crab at the fish market

1. Soft-shelled crab
Moeche are soft crabs that have shed their exo-skeleton and can be fried and eaten whole.

2. Mantis shrimps
Found in the Adriatic, these sweet-tasting crayfish are typically served boiled or chilled.

3. Goby fish
This tiny fish lives in the muddy sediment of the lagoon. Venetians cook them whole in risotto.

4. Spider crab
A monstrous crab with a red spiny shell that grows to 20 cm (7.8 inches) long. They taste best between October and December.

5. Octopus
Folpetti or musky octopus are a popular snack served year-round either fried, boiled or battered.

6. Schie
This small brown shrimp is a delicacy, and is traditionally served on polenta.

7. Scallops
King and queen scallops (capesante and canestrelli) are abundant across the Adriatic Sea.

8. Baby squid
The lagoon is a nursery for squid which are considered a delicacy.

9. Anchovies
A mainstay of the Venetian diet, alici or acciughe are often served raw or added to other dishes for flavour.

10. Clams
Traditional Venetian clams come in two forms: vongole veraci (small round-shelled clams) or cannelli (long, thin razor clams).

SOUVENIRS

1 Homewares
If you visit magnificent Ca'Rezzonico *(p53)*, you'll note the maximalist style of Venetian interiors swathed in damask, full of carved and painted wooden furniture, hung with glass chandeliers and fitted with brass and bronze decorations. Find your own smart homewares in Venice's abundant antique shops and stores such as Caigo da Mar *(p91)* and Valese Fonditore *(p91)*.

2 Wine
Venetian Doges drank golden-hued wine made from the Dorona grape grown on the island of Mazzorbo *(p119)*, which you can still taste at Venissa *(p123)*. Other city wine bars, like Estro *(p72)*, serve a wealth of first-class Veneto wines such as Soave, Garganega, Amarone, Valpolicella and bubbly Prosecco.

3 Masks
Masks were integral to the Venetian Carnival *(p80)*, enabling participants to remain anonymous while enjoying scandalous entertainments. Made from papier mâché, they evolved into a high art form taking different shapes and characters, such as *arlecchino* (Harlequin). Why not make your own at Ca' Macana *(p69)*?

A handmade mask, worn during the Carnival

4 Jewellery
On the eastern side of the Rialto Bridge, Ruga dei Oresi (the "street of goldsmiths") attests to the jewellery industry that thrived here. It was distinguished by the fine technique of Venetian goldsmiths and their use of coloured gems and brilliant enamelwork. Jewellers Sigfrido Cipolato *(sigfridocipolato.com)*, Simionato Enrico *(langolodorovenezia.it)* and Nardi *(nardi-venezia.com)* continue the tradition.

5 Paper
Venice was well-established in the publishing industry in the 15th century and is home to one of Italy's oldest public libraries, the Biblioteca Marciana *(p32)*. Since then, the city has had a love affair with printing, bookbinding, hand stamping and embossing, and artful paper marbling. Paolo Olbi *(olbi.atspace. com)* is the city's most experienced paper artisans while Legatoria Polliero *(295 Campo dei Frari)* turns out fabulous artifacts wrapped in equally fabulous marbled papers.

6 Shoes and Slippers
The Venetian shoemaking confraternity dates back to 1200 CE, and incorporated the factories on the Brenta Riviera, where wealthy Venetians had summer homes. You might spot gondolieri sporting furlane, which are made of colourful velvet, silk, linen or brocade, and have a rubber sole made from recycled bicycle tyres.

7 Textiles
It's true: Venice has an obsession with artisan textiles. Historic fabric houses producing handmade silk-velvet, damask and brocade include Luigi Bevilacqua *(p91)*, Fortuny *(p88)* and Rubelli *(rubelli.com)*. Meanwhile, designers such as Chiarastella Cattana *(chiarastellacattana.com)* employ age-old techniques in contemporary designs to progress the art further.

Colourful glassware made on the island of Murano

8 Glassware

For nearly a century, the Venetian island of Murano (p121) has been synonymous with the production of crystal and glassmaking. Continuing that thousand-year legacy, furnaces and workshops on the Fondamenta dei Vetrai continue to turn out winged goblets, etched mirrors and multi-tentacled chandeliers. Impress your guests back home with a genuine *millefiori* paperweight.

9 Eyewear

Given Venice's expertise in glassmaking, it's hardly surprising that its makers were pioneers of reading glasses in the 13th century. The tradition continues today in specialist stores like Ottica Vascellari (*otticavascellari.it*), where optometrists can fit you with a handcrafted frame to fit your face, personal style and even your prescription within 24–48 hours.

10 Fashion

The Venetian Republic was a fabulous arena for designers and artisans who fashioned the most glamorous dresses, suits and lace accessories in Europe. The island of Burano (p120) still maintains its delicate lace tradition while Fortuny continues to turn out its rare Delphic silk dresses.

TOP 10 FACTS ABOUT MURANO GLASS

1. The First Glassblower
The first Glass Master in Venice was bottle-maker Dominicus Phiolarius, who was recorded in 982 CE.

2. Trading Secrets Was Treason
Glassblowing techniques were considered trade secrets and any glassblower who left Venice was guilty of treason.

3. A Noble Profession
In 1376 it was decreed that glassblowers' daughters could marry into Venice's wealthiest families.

4. Laws for Gem Fraud
As coloured glass became more brilliant, laws were enacted to prohibit women wearing fake glass jewels which might suggest a higher social class.

5. Better Than Money
Between 1400 and 1700, Europeans trading in India and the African and American continents used Murano glass beads as currency.

6. Seed Beads
Seed beads are as small as the head of a needle and were produced in their billions to embroider dresses and jewellery.

7. Pioneering Mirrors
In the 15th century Angelo Barovier – the finest glassblower in Murano – discovered how to make perfectly clear glass, *cristallo Veneziano*. Thus the glass mirror was born.

8. Sculptural Chandeliers
The iconic Venetian chandelier is made up of hundreds of individually handblown pieces.

9. Seeing the Stars
The first glass telescope was made using Murano glass in 1609 for Galileo Galilei, marking the start of the Scientific Revolution.

10. Taxed Raw Materials
When the Habsburgs conquered Venice (1815–1835), they taxed the importation of raw materials needed for glassmaking.

VENICE FOR FREE

1 Basilica di San Marco
Entry to the city's main church *(p22)*, plastered with glittering Byzantine mosaics, is free of charge. Modelled on Saint Sophia in Constantinople, the basilica is a glorious reflection of the city's Byzantine connection. The cavernous building has walls lined with artistically cut rock-slabs and superb geometric patterns on the floor.

2 Take a Free Walking Tour
Every morning and afternoon, free guided walking tours *(venicefree walkingtour.com)* in English are organized from Campo Santi Apostoli in Cannaregio. Knowledgeable volunteers accompany visitors on short walks through places off the beaten track. It is essential to book ahead to ensure a spot.

3 Art Night
Concerts, exhibitions, lectures, demonstrations of craft techniques and videos are on all over the city on a set night in June *(artnightvenezia.it)*, all organized by the City Council and Ca' Foscari University. Reservations are necessary for some events.

4 Isola di San Michele Cemetery
An island circled by tall brick walls and dotted with cypress trees houses the city's monumental cemetery *(p119)*. Even if you have little interest in paying

Isola di San Michele Cemetery, built in the early 1800s

homage at the tombs of notable residents Igor Stravinsky, Diaghilev or Joseph Brodsky, it's a pleasant spot simply for strolling around.

5 Free Museum Entry
On the first Sunday of each month, entry to all Italian state-run museums and galleries is free for all visitors. In Venice, this includes the Gallerie dell'Accademia, Galleria Franchetti alla Ca' d'Oro, Museo Archeologico, Museo d'Arte Orientale and Palazzo Grimani.

6 Watching the Boats Go By
Settle down on any canal edge, and enjoy the unique sight of people going about their day-to-day business by boat – rubbish

barges, transport floats, florist boats, taxi launches, to mention but a few. And the water is often shared by ducks and cormorants fishing. Choice spots are Punta della Dogana (p102), the Zattere (p101) and the main Cannaregio canal.

7 T Fondaco dei Tedeschi Rooftop Terrace

📍 P3 🏠 Calle del Fontego dei Tedeschi, Rialto Bridge, S Marco
🕐 Hours vary, chech website
🌐 dfs.com

Located at the foot of the Rialto Bridge (p34), this modern department store is housed in the former main post office building, which has been transformed into luxury shops. The top of the building affords spectacular views – book a free visit online.

8 Museo della Musica

📍 N6 🏠 Chiesa di S Maurizio, Campo S Maurizio, S Marco
🌐 museodellamusica.com

This fascinating museum, housed in a church, offers free entrance, allowing visitors to admire its historical collection of remarkable musical instruments dating back to the time of Vivaldi.

9 Castello Giardini Pubblici

Located in the Castello district, these gardens (p114) were laid out in the late 1800s by French occupiers, as quickly becomes clear from the style. Shade and benches can be enjoyed to rest your weary feet, while the children let off steam in the playground.

10 Free Concerts

In neighbourhood halls and churches, orchestras and choirs from Italy and overseas often hold concerts, which are free to spectators. To find out about these events in advance, check the street posters affixed to the city walls.

Relaxing on the banks of the Grand Canal, Venice's great waterway

FESTIVALS AND EVENTS

1 Carnival
Feb–Mar, concluding on Shrove Tue

This 10-day extravaganza takes over the city as a countdown to Lent. The streets mill with costumed and masked local "nobility" and visitors. It starts with the Volo dell'Angelo (flight of the angel), when either an acrobat or a cardboard dove is launched from the Campanile in Piazza San Marco, showering onlookers with confetti. The grand finale is the explosive Mardi Gras.

2 Su e Zo per i Ponti
Late Mar/Apr: 4th Sun in Lent
w suezo.it

Anyone can join this non-competitive walk or run "up and down the bridges". Some official routes include an 11-km (6.5-mile) route that runs over 39 bridges and a 5-km (3-mile) route that stretches across 18 bridges. All participants receive a medal on finishing.

3 Festa della Sensa
May: Ascension Day

Head for the Riviera di San Nicolò at the Lido (p125) to watch this ancient ceremony of "Venice wedding to the Sea". A costumed "doge" casts a ring into the sea amid a procession of celebratory boats. Symbolizing Venice's maritime supremacy, La Sensa has been staged since Venice took over Istria and Dalmatia in 997 CE.

4 Vogalonga
May: Sun after Ascension

A colourful armada of rowing craft from all over the world embarks on a 32-km (20-mile) non-competitive route around the lagoon's scattered islands. The "Long Row" is a great experience for both participants and onlookers, who line the Canale di Cannaregio towards midday to cheer on the breathtaking final stretch down the Grand Canal.

5 Biennale Art Exhibition
Jun–Nov **w** labiennale.org

The world's leading international art bonanza is held on a two-yearly basis. The leafy gardens in eastern Castello are the principal venue, supplemented by the Corderie building in the Arsenale.

6 Festa del Redentore
Mid-Jul

People hop on to all available watercraft, decorated with paper lanterns and

The *Serenissima* ceremonial boat during the Festa della Sensa

Costumed revellers wearing masks during the Carnival

greenery, for a feast of roast duck and watermelon, followed by a midnight fireworks display. It all takes place over a Saturday afternoon, near Palladio's church on Giudecca (p125) to commemorate the end of the 1576 plague. For those getting there on foot, a temporary pontoon bridge stretches from the Zattere over the Giudecca Canal.

7 Festa di San Rocco
16 Aug
The feast day of St Roch, the French saint adopted by the confraternity for alleviating the 1576–7 plague, is celebrated each year at the Scuola Grande di San Rocco (p95).

8 Regata Storica
1st Sun in Sep
The word regatta originated in Venice. At the year's most spectacular event, ornately decorated boats propelled by costumed oarsmen parade down the Grand Canal with passengers dressed as historical dignitaries. A series of furiously contested regattas follows.

9 Venice Marathon
Late Oct
Runners from all parts of the globe begin this classic – not to mention beautiful – 42-km (26-mile) race at Villa Pisani on the Brenta waterway, across the causeway to Venice, the Zattere and San Marco, to finish near the public gardens in Castello. Other race routes are 21 km (13 miles) and 10 km (6.5 miles) long.

10 Festa della Salute
21 Nov
Venetians make a pilgrimage to Longhena's church (p54) every winter in memory of the devastating plague of 1630–31, which wiped out almost one third of Venice's population. To commemorate the end of the epidemic, the whole area assumes a festive atmosphere with stalls selling candy floss and balloons.

TOP 10
SPORTS IN VENICE

Sailing in the lagoon

1. Sailing
Yachtsmen gather at the marina on San Giorgio Maggiore island, which looks directly over the lagoon.

2. Cycling
Illegal in Venice itself, though you'll see kids zooming around. It is allowed in the Lido, where you can rent a bike from a cycle shop on the main street.

3. Rowing
Immensely popular Venetian pastime practised standing up. Join the oldest club, Canottieri Bucintoro.

4. Swimming
Head for the Lido or the indoor pools at Sacca Fisola and Sant'Alvise.

5. In-Line Skating
There's a small rink at Sant'Elena in Castello, otherwise stick to the Lido pavements.

6. Golf
The well-reputed 18-hole course at the Alberoni is on the south of the Lido.

7. Tennis
The Lido's tennis courts are open to visitors. Select hotels can arrange lessons for guests, too.

8. Jogging
The city's stone paving isn't great for your knees, so try the public parks, where runners train for the Venice Marathon and shorter races.

9. Gyms
Private gyms with state-of-the-art equipment, located in the city, can be found online.

10. Football
The home team Venezia plays at Stadio Pier Luigi Penzo, their stadium in Sant'Elena, on Sundays.

FREQUENTLY ASKED QUESTIONS

1 How Does the House Numbering System Work?

Venice is divided into six neighbourhoods (*sestieri*), each of which has a unique numbering system starting from a designated first house. Within each *sestieri*, numbers follow the alleyways, taking in branch streets and courtyards.

2 What Do the Buildings Stand On?

Thousands of tree trunks support Venice's palaces. Shipped from Croatia and the Dolomites, they were driven into the *caranto* (clay mud) of the lagoon and topped with slabs of impermeable Istrian marble. As the wooden pylons are underwater and not exposed to oxygen they have hardened like fossils and do not decay.

3 What Are the MoSE Floodgates??

A mobile flood barrier, MoSE (Modulo Sperimentale Elettromeccanico or Experimental Electromechanical Module) consists of 78 inflatable barriers (30 m/98 ft high, 20 m/65 ft wide), which are raised when high tides reach dangerous levels and threaten to flood the city.

4 How Can I Avoid the Crowds?

Despite reports of over-tourism in Venice, it's not difficult to avoid the crowds with some creative thinking. Book accommodation in quiet Santa Croce, Cannaregio and Castello, or stay on lagoon islands like Murano, Burano and the sunny Lido. All are within easy reach of San Marco by public transport.

5 How Deep Is the Lagoon?

The depth of the lagoon varies. Most canals are up to 2 m (6.5 ft) deep, but the Grand Canal is around 5 m (16 ft) deep, while the lagoon has shallow areas where mussels, oysters and shrimp thrive. The deepest points are the 15-m- (49-ft-) deep Giudecca Canal and the 21-m (68-ft-) deep Canale dei Petroli, which are navigable channels dredged for shipping.

6 Where Can You Swim?

Swimming in the canal is forbidden and incurs a hefty fine. After all, these are Venice's "roads" and are full of boat traffic. You can swim off a few island "beaches" on more distant lagoon islands such as Sant'Erasmo and Poveglia. The best place to swim, though, is off the sandy beaches of the Lido, which face the Adriatic Sea.

7 How Can I Give Back to Venice?

The best way to truly give back to Venice is to embrace slow travel, such as enjoying a longer stay. You can also

Passengers on board a vaporetto (waterbus) in Torcello

contribute directly by booking into locally run accommodation – consider the socially minded Fairbnb *(fairbnb.coop)*, which was founded by a Venetian – and eating and shopping in locally run restaurants and artisan shops.

8 Does Everyone Have a Boat?

Although there is an impressive array of boats lining Venice's canals, barely half of Venetians own a boat, because they're expensive to maintain and dock. Most boats in Venice are owned by those in the transport and tourism businesses, as well as working fishers.

9 Is Venice Still Sinking?

Theoretically, the sinking came to a halt when the industries in Marghera (an industrial zone on the mainland) stopped pumping out groundwater – but the admission of large cruise ships into the lagoon, the relative rising sea level and the impact of climate change is slowly turning the lagoon into a bay.

10 How Do You Get Around Venice?

The most efficient way to get around is on foot. Otherwise, the public transport system of vaporetti (waterbuses) is extremely efficient and operates like a metro with tickets dispensed at automatic machines by the docks. There are also three *traghetto* (ferry) points along the Grand Canal where people can board a gondola for €2.

A house with its number above the door in San Maggiore

TOP 10
WAYS TO HELP VENICE

1. Take a Tour
You'll appreciate this unique city all the more with the thoughtful guidance of one of Venice's best guides *(bestveniceguides.it)*.

2. Bring Your Own Bottle
Venice has over 150 public water wells dotted throughout the city *(venicetapwater.com)* from where you can drink filtered rainwater.

3. Enjoy Venetian "fast food"
Support Venetian traditions in *cicheti* (tapas) bars which serve open-topped snacks and regional wine.

4. Respect Local Life
Respect Venetians' space by avoiding picnicking in public squares, blocking bridges and sitting on local steps.

5. Follow Rubbish Rules
Did you know that all rubbish in Venice is hand-collected and taken out by boat? You can help by putting litter in the correct bins.

6. Avoid Rush Hour
Like all urbanites, Venetians just want to get home after a long day's work. Steer clear of the vaporetto (waterbus) during peak times.

7. Travel Smart
Motorboats can contribute to the damage of city foundations. Avoid asking drivers to speed and take public transport where you can.

8. Shop Local, Shop Well
Venice is full of gifted artisans creating unique handmade goods. Support them in their work and you'll take home enviable souvenirs.

9. Authentic Venice
Sebastian Fagarazzi and Valeria Duflot are co-founders of Venezia Autentica *(veneziaautentica.com)*, an open source platform showcasing a variety of the best produce and items that Venice has to offer.

10. Support Save Venice
Become a supporter of Venice's leading non-profit, Save Venice, which is devoted to preserving the city's artistic heritage.

AREA BY AREA

Burano island, the Northern Lagoon

SAN MARCO

Venice's smallest but foremost *sestiere* (district), named after the city's patron saint, is bounded by the Grand Canal on all but one side, with a high number of stately palaces in the area. It revolves around Piazza San Marco and the majestic Doge's Palace, the political and legal core of the city until the 18th century. Running off the square are the Mercerie and Calle Larga XXII Marzo, offering wall-to-wall designer shopping. But beyond that San Marco has a residential air, with a great range of places to eat. Don't hesitate to wander down minor alleyways: surprises include unusual wellheads and many craft workshops.

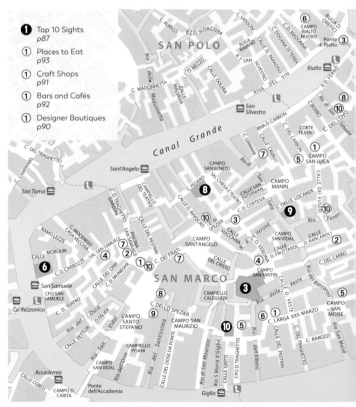

1. Top 10 Sights
   p87
1. Places to Eat
   p93
1. Craft Shops
   p91
1. Bars and Cafés
   p92
1. Designer Boutiques
   p90

For places to stay in this area, see p148

1 Piazza San Marco

This square *(p30)* was named by Napoleon as "the finest drawing room in Europe." The monuments here showcase Venice's history, from the Torre dell'Orologio (a Renaissance-style clock) to a pair of 18th-century carved lions on the site of a former vegetable market.

2 Mercerie

🗺 Q4

The elegance of Venice is evident on this main thoroughfare linking Rialto and Piazza San Marco. *Mercerie* means "haberdasher's", but these days it is home to designer fashion outlets. Just below the ornate Torre dell'Orologio

A concert at Teatro La Fenice, Venice's oldest theatre

archway is a sculpted female figure commemorating a housewife who lived here rent-free as a reward for inadvertently knocking a mortar into the street, killing a revolutionary leader and so halting the short-lived Bajamonte Tiepolo revolt in 1310.

3 Teatro La Fenice

🗺 N5 🏛 Campo S Fantin
🌐 teatrolafenice.it 🎫

Long masked in scaffolding since a 1996 arson attack left it gutted, the historic "Phoenix" theatre rose from the flames in 2003. Selva's 1792 opera house has staged countless world premieres including Rossini's *Tancredi* in 1813, five operas commissioned of Verdi, most notably *Rigoletto* and *La Traviata*, and works by Stravinsky and Luigi Nono. Legendary divas such as Maria Callas and Dame Joan Sutherland have sung in this glorious setting *(p71)*.

4 Basilica di San Marco

Built on a Greek cross plan, and crowned with five huge domes, this is the third church *(p22)* to stand on this site. In 1807, it succeeded San Pietro in Castello as the cathedral of Venice. Embellished over a period of six centuries, it features mosaics, marble and carvings and served as a fitting location for ceremonies of the Republic. It was here that the elected doge was presented to the city following his election. This is also where sea captains came to pray for protection before embarking on epic voyages.

GLASSMAKING

Venetian glasswork exquisitely decorates chandeliers, chalices and mirrors and has long been in demand the world over, especially during the 16th century. Although the industry moved to Murano in 1295 as a safety measure against fire, there are still many furnaces around the San Marco district that welcome visitors.

5 Campo San Bartolomeo

P3

The statue of celebrated Venetian playwright Carlo Goldoni scrutinizes the milling crowds on this crossroads square. Strategically placed for a host of inviting bars crammed into the alleys radiating off it, "San Bartolo" is a hang-out spot for the city's young and trendy. The northern end is occupied by the former post office building (now housing luxury shops), once home to Venice's German community (p57). They worshipped in the Chiesa di San Bartolomeo.

6 Palazzo Grassi

L5 **Campo S Samuele, S Marco 3231** **10am–7pm Wed–Mon (last adm: 6pm)** **palazzograssi.it**

Set on the Grand Canal, Palazzo Grassi dates back to 1740, when a wealthy merchant family commissioned Giorgio Massari to design the building. It is now home to the François Pinault collection, housing contemporary masterpieces by Jeff Koons, Damien Hirst and Michelangelo Pistoletto. It stands alongside picturesque Campo San Samuele, which features a graceful Veneto-Byzantine bell tower. Its sister gallery is Punta della Dogana (p102).

7 Doge's Palace

The seat of the Venetian government from the 9th century until the fall of the Republic in 1797, the Doge's Palace (p26) was the official residence of the Venetian ruler, known as the doge. It started life as a fortified castle in the 9th century, but this and several subsequent buildings were destroyed by a series of fires. A Gothic masterpiece, the bulk of the pink marble building appears perched on loggias and arcades of white Istrian stone. Allegorical historical paintings embellish the walls and ceilings of the halls and chambers. These rooms are testament to the glory of the Venetian Republic.

8 Museo Fortuny

N4 **Campo S Benedetto, S Marco 3780** **10am–5pm Wed–Mon (Apr–Oct: to 6pm; last adm: an hour before closing)** **visitmuve.it**

Flamboyant Spanish artist and theatrical stage designer Mariano Fortuny y Madrazo (1871–1950) adopted Venice as his home and muse, and transformed this 15th-century palace in Gothic-Venetian style into an atelier. The building retains rooms created by Fortuny himself and visitors can admire Fortuny's gorgeous velvets, his famous pleated silk dresses, some 150 paintings, lamps, a remarkable stage curtain and fascinating 19th-century photographs. The museum also hosts temporary exhibitions.

The impressive interior of the Palazzo Grassi

Beautiful external spiral staircase of
Palazzo Contarini del Bovolo

9 Palazzo Contarini del Bovolo

📍 P4 🏛 Corte dei Risi, S Marco 4303
🕐 Nov–Feb: 9:30am–5:30pm daily
(last adm: 5pm); Mar–Oct: 10am–
6pm daily (last adm: 5:30pm)
🌐 gioiellinascostidivenezia.it 📶

Often used as a film set, this fine
15th-century palace with its beautiful
external "snail-shell" staircase (*bovolo*
means snail in Venetian) is squeezed
into a diminutive square deep in San
Marco. Visitors can climb the winding
steps of the staircase, a blend of
Renaissance, Gothic and Byzantine
styles, via five floors of loggias to a
dome sheltering a splendid belvedere.
From here there are magical panoramic views over the city's rooftops.

10 Chiesa di Santa Maria del Giglio

📍 N6 🏛 Campo S Maria del Giglio,
S Marco 3231 🕐 10:30am–5pm
Mon–Sat 🌐 chorusvenezia.org 📶

Opening on to a lovely square next
to the Grand Canal, this church is a
further example of Venetian Baroque
extravagance. Commissioned by
the Barbaro family, its façade exalts
their generations of maritime and
political triumphs, with crests, galleys
and statues. Works of art inside the
church include Venice's only canvas
by Rubens, depicting a Madonna and
child. Tintoretto's contributions are
the Evangelists on the organ doors.

A DAY IN SAN MARCO

Morning

Visit the **Doge's Palace** (*p26*)
on **Piazza San Marco** (*p30*).
Must-sees at the palace include
the Sala del Senato, Sala del
Maggior Consiglio, prisons and
the Bridge of Sighs. Then take a
break for coffee in the modern
café in the palace's former stables
and watch the gondolas glide
past the glassed-in doorway.

Time your visit to **Basilica di San
Marco** (*p22*) for midday, to catch
the mosaics illuminated by huge
spotlights so they glitter to their
utmost. The tiles were laid at
angles to catch the light.

Have lunch at **Harry's Bar**
(*p35*), as Hemingway's hero did
in *Across the River and Into
the Trees*. Order the *carpaccio*
(wafer-thin slices of raw beef)
invented here by Cipriani (*p74*).

Afternoon

The **Mercerie** (*p87*) is shopper's
heaven, packed with international
high-fashion stores from Benetton
to Cartier, and classy souvenir
glass and hand-crafted paper
workshops. For yet more, cross
over to Calle Larga XXII Marzo for
designer delights such as **Bulgari**
(*p90*) and **Cartier** jewellery (*p90*).

Return to **Piazza San Marco** (*p30*)
to enjoy the views over Venice and
the lagoon from the Campanile at
dusk. Watch the sun set behind the
basilica, while enjoying a Bellini
aperitivo at **Caffè Florian** (*p30*).

Designer Boutiques

Innovative paper cone vases at L'Isola - Carlo Moretti

1. L'Isola – Carlo Moretti
📍 M5 🚇 Calle delle Botteghe, S Marco 2970
Exhibited in galleries all over the world, this is contemporary glass at its most innovative. Moretti's trademarks are "paper cone" vases, tumblers and huge sculptures.

2. Frette
📍 P5 🚇 Frezzeria, S Marco 1725
Since 1860, Frette has been importing top-grade cotton from Egypt and transforming it into towels and custom-made household linen.

3. Eredi di Jovon
📍 P3 🚇 Ponte Rialto, S Marco 5325
This family-run jewellery store creates traditional and unique Venetian and Murano glass pieces. Their private museum is open to visitors by appointment.

4. Ottico Urbani
📍 E4 🚇 San Marco Frezzeria, S Marco 1280
The Urbani brothers have been designing eyewear since 1953, creating frames from unique materials such as fabric and wood. Their designs are a favourite with celebrities visiting the city for the International Film Festival.

5. Cartier
📍 P5 🚇 Calle San Moisè, S Marco 1474
The fortress-like premises of these world-famous French jewellers gleam with gold, precious stones and well-crafted handbags and watches.

6. MaxMara
📍 P3 🚇 Campo S Salvador, S Marco 5033
This family company has been designing fashionable clothes and accessories for city girls since 1951.

7. Bulgari
📍 P5 🚇 Salizzada San Moisè, S Marco 1494
Striking contemporary jewellery, watches, accessories and Rosenthal porcelain are sold here.

8. Fratelli Rossetti
📍 P3 🚇 Campo S Salvador, S Marco 4800
This family-run firm was established in 1953 and is known worldwide for the superb Italian elegance it displays in the likes of shoes, belts, bags and jackets.

9. Fendi
📍 P5 🚇 Frezzeria, S Marco 1225
Go straight to the source for flamboyant frocks and shoes for special occasions and crazily beaded bags, all sporting the "double-F" Fendi mark.

10. Giuliana Longo
📍 P3 🚇 Calle del Lovo, S Marco 4813
Founded in 1902, this tiny shop manufactures and sells elegant panama, carnival and gondoliers' hats. Fascinators are available, too.

Craft Shops

1. I Muschieri
P5 Calle Frezzaria, S Marco 1178 muschieri.com

A treat for perfume lovers, this small shop is run by two famous Venetian sisters, who create bespoke fragrances for customers.

2. BAC Art Studio
M5 Calle delle Botteghe, S Marco 3451 bacart.com

This art gallery sells attractive and affordable etchings and prints of Venice by artists Baruffaldi and Cadore.

3. Max Art
P5 Frezzeria, S Marco 1232 antoniasautter.it

Commedia dell'arte marionettes, musical puppet theatres and glittering Carnival masks are available here for sale or hire.

4. Caigo Da Mar
M5 Salizzada San Samuele, S Marco 3157/A caigodamar.com

This speciality boutique offers luxurious home decor items and jewellery.

5. Bevilacqua
N5 Campo S Maria del Giglio, S Marco 2520 luigi-bevilacqua.com

Handmade velvet and silk cushions and tapestries are a feast for the eyes at this small branch of the historic Italian fabric shop.

Entrance to the luxury furnishing store Bevilacqua

A copperleaf lamp at Venetia Studium

6. Venetia Studium
P5 Calle Larga XXII Marzo, S Marco 2425 fortuny.uk

Exquisite hanging silk lamps of Fortuny design are reproduced with hand-painted patterning and glass beading here.

7. Rigattieri
M5 Calle dei Frati, S Marco 3532/36

Ceramics enthusiasts must not miss this extraordinary shop of beautiful pottery. It has been run by the same family since it was founded – at this address – in 1938, and the focus is firmly on high-quality pieces.

8. Valese Fonditore
Q4 Calle Fiubera, S Marco 793 valese.it/fonderia-artistica-valese-venezia

The Valese family foundry has been creating their animals, lamps and door knockers in brass and bronze since 1913. Examples of their work can even be found in Buckingham Palace and The White House.

9. Le Botteghe della Solidarietà
P3 Salizzada Pio X, S Marco 5164 bottegadellasolidarieta.it

A kaleidoscopic display of handwoven shawls from India and musical instruments from African countries are part of an enterprise that is intended to guarantee artisans a just income.

10. Daniela Ghezzo Segalin a Venezia
P4 Calle dei Fuseri, S Marco 4365 danielaghezzo.it

In addition to the brocade slippers and bizarre footwear with built-in toes, special-order shoes are also hand-crafted here.

Bars and Cafés

1. Pasticceria Marchini Time
📍 P4 🏠 Campo S Luca, S Marco 4589
A paradise for those with a sweet tooth, Marchini is one of the oldest *pasticcerie* in the city. Orange and pistachio chocolates come in Venetian mask shapes.

2. I Rusteghi
📍 Q3 🏠 Corte del Tintor, S Marco 5513
Tucked away behind Campo San Bartolomeo, this *osteria* is run by a friendly sommelier-owner. It has an excellent selection of wines and *cicchetti* (bar snacks).

3. Caffè Brasilia
📍 N4 🏠 Rio Terrà Assassini, S Marco 3658
Tuck into a huge, fresh fruit salad smothered with yogurt or a *tramezzino* (sandwich) in this quiet side-alley café, with tables inside and a few outside. The coffee's good, too.

4. Bar al Theatro
📍 N5 🏠 Campo S Fantin, S Marco 1916 🌐 altheatro.it
Next door to the renowned Teatro la Fenice (*p87*), this legendary venue offers outdoor seating on a patio. Alternatively, go inside to the bar and munch a toasted sandwich.

5. Suso Gelatoteca
📍 Q3 🏠 Sotoportego de la Bissa 5453 🌐 suso.gelatoteca.it
Try the peanut ice cream at this gorgeous *gelateria* (*p73*). Expect silky, smooth scoops and delicious vegan options. It's expensive, but worth it.

6. Bacarando
📍 P3 🏠 Corte dell'Orso, S Marco 5495 🌐 bacarando.com
This great spot offers bar snacks at aperitivo time, but also has an elegant restaurant. Wednesday nights see the addition of live music.

7. Enoteca Al Volto
📍 D4 🏠 Calle Cavalli, San Marco 4081 🌐 enotecaalvolto.com
Located near the town hall, this traditional *osteria* serves mouthwatering snacks such as the Venetian *cicchetti*. Popular with the locals, it fills up quickly on weekdays.

8. Le Café
📍 M5 🏠 Campo S Stefano, S Marco 2797 🌐 lecafevenezia.com
Have a fresh orange juice or cappuccino and pastry as you watch life go by in the square. The usual hot dishes are available, and there is also a *pasticceria* offering tasty tarts and pastries.

9. Rosa Salva
📍 Q4 🏠 Ponte Ferai, S Marco 950
Come here to enjoy fruit tarts that melt in the mouth, exquisite pastries and Venice's best panettone.

10. Bar all'Angolo
📍 M5 🏠 Campo Santo Stefano, S Marco 3464 🚫 Sun
Tourists and locals alike are unable to resist this great sandwich bar. Bag a table outside for a well-earned coffee or light lunch.

Pasticceria Marchini Time, known for its chocolate-shaped masks

Places to Eat

Outdoor tables in the garden at the La Caravella

You have the choice of eating at the bar or at a table outside. American Express credit card is not accepted.

1. La Caravella
Q P5 **△** Via XXII Marzo, S Marco 2399 **W** restaurantlacaravella.com · €€€
Resembling a caravel sailing ship, this place has trestle tables. Try the Venetian dishes with a modern twist here.

2. Grand Canal
Q Q6 **△** Calle Vallaresso, S Marco 1332 **C** 041 520 02 11 · €€€
Part of Hotel Monaco, Grand Canal offers stylish dining all year round. The extensive menu features Venetian cuisine and fish dishes.

3. Do Forni
Q Q4 **△** Calle Specchieri, S Marco 468 **W** doforni.it · €€€
This restaurant has a long list of celebrity guests. Seasonal specialities and an extensive wine list are on offer.

4. Rosticceria San Bartolomeo
Q P3 **△** Calle della Bissa, S Marco 5424 **C** 041 522 35 69 · €
Also known as the Gislon, this place serves great *mozzarella in carozza*, a deep-fried cheese sandwich.

5. Osteria Leon Bianco
Q P4 **△** Campo S Luca, S Marco 4153 **C** 041 522 11 80 · €
This spot is a great choice for grilled meats and fish or a plate of lasagne

6. Trattoria alla Madonna
Q P3 **△** Calle della Madonna, S Polo 594 **C** 7 Jan–end-Jan & Wed, 25 Dec **W** ristoranteallamadonna.com · €€
A well-known, bustling restaurant, perfect for traditional seafood. Seafood risotto is a speciality.

7. Al Bacareto
Q M5 **△** Calle delle Botteghe, S Marco 3447 **C** Sun **W** bacareto.it · €
A Venetian stalwart since 1971, Al Bacareto serves typical local dishes. Try the *bigoli in salsa* (spaghetti with anchovy and onion purée).

8. Osteria Enoteca San Marco
Q P5 **△** Frezzeria, S Marco 1610 **W** osteriasanmarco.it · €€
An exemplary wine list accompanies the tasty bar snacks and a small, but perfectly formed, menu.

9. Ristorante A Beccafico
Q M5 **△** Campo S Stefano, S Marco 2801 **C** 041 527 48 79 · €€€
The menu here blends Sicilian dishes with Venetian cuisine and includes pasta, meat and fish, plus fabulous desserts.

10. Acqua Pazza
Q N5 **△** Campo Sant'Angelo, S Marco 3808/10 **C** 7 Jan–7 Feb & Mon end-Nov–early-Dec **W** venice acquapazza.com · €€€
Amalfi cuisine, including Neapolitan pizza, pasta and fish dishes, feature at this fine-dining restaurant.

SAN POLO AND SANTA CROCE

Venice's greatest concentration of sights can be found in these neighbouring districts, at the geographical heart of the city, having grown around the ancient core of Rialto where the first inhabitants settled. Here, glorious churches, landmark monuments and breathtaking palaces are all saturated in history. Essential sights include Santa Maria Gloriosa dei Frari, the Scuola Grande di San Rocco, where Tintoretto demonstrated his genius on sumptuous canvases, and the morning bustle of Rialto market, the go-to place for seasonal fruits, vegetables and fish since medieval times. The squares of San Polo and San Giacomo dall'Orio are both full of cafés and benches for resting weary feet.

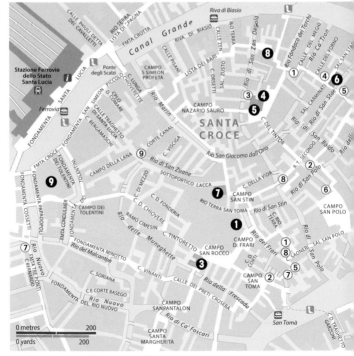

For places to stay in this area, see p148

Gothic church of Santa Maria Glorisa dei Frari

1 Santa Maria Gloriosa dei Frari

Known by all simply as the Frari (a corruption of *Frati*, meaning "friars"), this huge, plain Gothic church (p40) dwarfs the eastern section of San Polo. The first church was built by Fransiscan friars during 1250–1338, but was replaced by a larger building, which was completed by the mid-15th century. The interior is striking for its sheer size and for the quality of its works of art. These include masterpieces by Titan and Giovanni Bellini, as well as Donatello's famous John the Baptist and a number of imposing monuments to famous Venetians. The campanile, set into the left transept of the church, is the second largest in the city.

2 The Rialto

This area (p42) is home to some of Venice's most iconic sights. The fresh produce and fish markets have enlivened it since medieval times. The Rialto is also home to the most famous bridge on the Canal Grande, the Rialto Bridge, which provides impressive views of the city.

3 Scuola Grande di San Rocco

🅚 K4 🏠 Campo S Rocco, S Polo 3052 🕒 9:30am–5:30pm daily 🗓 1 Jan, 25 Dec 🖥 scuolagrandesanrocco.org ♿

The early Renaissance façade of this historic building, home to masterpieces by Tintoretto, is a marvel of intertwined sculpted stone wreaths and crouching elephants dwarfed by stately columns. The Istrian stone facing is embedded with burgundy porphyry and green- and cream-veined marble inserts. Designed by Bartolomeo Bon in 1517 and added to by Scarpagnino among others, the building was home to one of the city's foremost confraternities, established in 1478, and honoured with an annual visit by the doge.

4 Campo San Giacomo dall'Orio

🅚 L2

This square, well off the beaten track, sports plane trees, benches for relaxing and patches of grass. The surrounding palaces are home to Venice University's architectural faculties. The abundance of restaurants and coffee shops make it very inviting, and there's no lack of subjects for photographers or artists.

SAN POLO

Canal Grande

1 Top 10 Sights p95
1 Places to Eat p99
1 Craft Shops p98

5 Chiesa di San Giacomo dall'Orio

📍 L2 🏛 Campo S Giacomo dall'Orio, S Croce ⏰ 10am–5pm Mon–Sat 🌐 chorusvenezia.org 🔗

Do not miss this unusual church. Founded in the 9th century, its Latin-cross shape features a marvellous 15th-century wood-beamed ceiling and a forest of colourful granite and black limestone columns from the Middle East, several of them loot from the Crusades. The floor merits close scrutiny for its multitude of fossils, while memorable paintings include Palma il Giovane's *Descent of Manna* (1580–81), left of the main altar, and a painted crucifix (1350) attributed to Paolo Veneziano.

6 Palazzo Mocenigo

📍 M2 🏛 Salizzada S Stae, S Croce 1992 ⏰ 10am–5pm Tue–Sun (Apr–Oct: 10am–6pm; last adm: 30 min before closing) 🚫 1 Jan, 1 May, 25 Dec 🌐 visitmuve.it 🔗

The richly furnished and frescoed rooms of this 18th-century patrician palace have showcases of historic fabrics and costumes, plus a fascinating history of perfumes. The Mocenigo family portrait gallery has a total of seven doges, topped in fame by Alvise I, the victor at the 1571 Battle of Lepanto against the Turks, which was crucial for the Republic.

Courtyard of the Scuola Grande di San Giovanni Evangelista

7 Scuola Grande di San Giovanni Evangelista

📍 L3 🏛 Campiello della Scuola, S Polo 2454 ⏰ 9:30am–1pm & 2–5:15pm daily 🌐 scuolasan giovanni.it 🔗

This erstwhile confraternity headquarters with a high-ceilinged upstairs hall is mostly used for conferences. The monumental staircase was the work of Coducci and the priceless reliquary contains a fragment of the True Cross, presented to the Scuola in 1369. The spectacular *Miracles of the Cross* cycle of paintings commissioned of Gentile Bellini and associates is now in the Accademia Galleries *(p38)*. The exterior courtyard has a fine sculptured portal screen completed in 1485 by Pietro Lombardo mounted with an eagle to symbolize St John.

8 Campo San Zan Degolà

📍 L1 🏛 Chiesa di San Giovanni Decollato ⏰ 9am–4pm Mon–Sat

People usually hurry through this square en route to the bus terminal, oblivious to its quiet charm. Interest starts with the curious loggia on the western canal edge, then there's the attractive plain church named for San Giovanni Decollato or St John the Beheaded, depicted with flowing curly locks in a stone bas-relief on the southern wall. Inside the simple

Colourful frescoed interior of Palazzo Mocenigo

Veneto-Byzantine building are lovely 13th-century frescoes, an unusual survivor for damp old Venice.

9 Giardino Papadopoli
J3

A leafy haven of twittering sparrows and flowerbeds close to Piazzale Roma and the car parks, these French-designed gardens date back to the 1800s when extravagant parties for the nobility were held here among various flower species and rare animals. Site of a demolished convent, it belonged to Corfu-born entrepreneurs, hence the Greek name. The public park was greatly reduced in size when the Rio Nuovo canal was excavated in 1932–3.

10 Ca' Pesaro Museo di Arte Orientale
N1 Fondamenta Ca' Pesaro, S Croce 2076 10am–5pm Tue–Sun (Apr–Oct: 10am–6pm; last adm: 30 min before closing) visitmuve.it

This impressive Oriental Art Collection is an eclectic mix of 19th-century curiosities from all over the Far East. Exhibits include armour, porcelain and costumes, lacquerwork boxes and musical instruments. The museum is on the third floor, above the modern art gallery in Ca' Pesaro (p63). A single ticket grants admission into the gallery and the museum.

SCUOLE GRANDI

The Venetian Scuole Grandi (literally "great schools") were charitable institutions of medieval origin, almost Masonic in organization. Some were religious-orientated lay confraternities, while others functioned as trade guilds. Up to 500 once operated, covering everyone from sausage-makers to cobblers. Several have survived, namely San Rocco and Carmini.

A DAY IN SAN POLO

Morning

Before wandering east to Campo San Polo, stop at the **Scuola Grande di San Rocco** (p94) to view Tintoretto's paintings. Have coffee at one of the local bars or at the attractive **Antica Birraria La Corte** (p99).

It's not far from here to the **Rialto** market (p95) for late-morning bargains of fresh produce, often nearing half-price when stall-holders are in a hurry to shut up shop. After that, enjoy a Grand Canal-side lunch. There is a string of restaurants spread along the **Riva del Vin** (p35), close to the foot of Rialto Bridge. Each displays live lobster and fish and has multilingual menus. In winter diners sit in see-through "tents" so that views of the canal and the procession of boats are ensured.

Afternoon

Head north and explore the craft and gift shops, lace, scarf and T-shirt stalls along Ruga Rialto and the old red-light area of **Rio Terrà Rampani** (p66).

Try to end up in pretty **Campo San Giacomo dall'Orio** (p95) for a pre-dinner drink at **Al Prosecco** wine bar (Campo S Giacomo dall'Orio, S Croce 1503; closed Sun). Ask for a delicious glass of the fruity red Refosco from Friuli and bocconcino con mortadella di cinghiale (bite-sized roll with sliced wild boar) to round off.

Craft Shops

1. Gilberto Penzo
M3 **Calle Seconda dei Saoneri, S Polo 2681** **Sun** **veniceboats.com**
A visit to this workshop with beautiful wooden models of traditional Venetian boats is a real treat. Many crafts come in DIY kit form.

2. Mazzon le Borse
L4 **Campiello S Tomà, S Polo 2807** **Sun**
Papà Piero has been making beautiful leather bags that last a lifetime since 1963. His family helps him in the workshop.

3. Marina e Susanna Sent
P2 **Sottoportego del Rialto, S Polo 70** **Sun & Mon** **marina esusannasent.com**
Come here for strikingly simple but exquisitely elegant necklaces and earrings in clear and coloured glass.

4. Piedàterre
P3 **S Polo 60** **piedàterre venezia.com**
This boutique, located near the Rialto Bridge, manufactures and sells traditional Venetian shoes and slippers. Their speciality is the friulane, or furlane, the rubber-soled gondolier slippers.

5. Sabbie e Nebbie
M4 **Calle dei Nomboli, S Polo 2768/A** **Sun**
Customers come to this boutique to purchase ceramics, notebooks and scarves from Japan, Nepal and India.

6. Attombri
P2 **Sottoportego degli Orefici, S Polo 65** **Sun** **attombri.com**
In an old covered passageway that has long been home to the Rialto Market goldsmiths, Attombri is run by two designer brothers who make limited-edition jewellery.

Intricate hand-painted masks at Tragicomica

7. Tragicomica
M4 **Calle dei Nomboli, S Polo 2800** **Sun** **tragicomica.it**
The result of 20 years of creating elaborate papier-mâché and leather masks and brocade costumes for Carnival, as well as theatrical productions, can be seen in this craft shop.

8. Cenerentola
C4 **Calle dei Saoneri, 2718/A S Polo** **Sun**
Venetian fabrics, lampshades and lamps to satisfy every taste are sold here.

9. Margherita Rossetto Ceramica
K2 **Corte Canal, S Croce 659** **Sun**
Eggcups, teapots and platters are some of the delightful hand-turned objects available here.

10. Gems of Venice
N3 **Ruga Rialto 1044, S Polo** **gemsofvenice.it/about**
At this boutique and workshop precious gemstones are transformed into works of art that can be worn.

Places to Eat

PRICE CATEGORIES

For a three-course meal for one with half a bottle of wine (or equivalent meal), taxes and extra charges.

€ under €40 €€ €40–60 €€€ over €60

1. La Zucca

📍L1 🏠 Ponte del Megio, S Croce 1762 🕒 Sun 🌐 lazucca.it · €€

Delicious vegetarian fare is served here, and there is also the promise of unforgettable chocolate desserts.

2. Da Fiore

📍M3 🏠 Calle dello Scaleter, S Polo 2202/A 🕒 Sun & L (except Sat), 3 weeks in Jan & Aug 🌐 ristorante dafiore.com · €€€

The exclusive Da Fiore is possibly one of Venice's best restaurants. For great views, reserve the outdoor table on the balcony. Book in advance.

3. Il Refolo

📍L2 🏠 Campo San Giacomo dall'Orio, S Croce 1459 🕒 Tue 🌐 il-refolo.business.site · €

Diners come to this great canalside spot for inexpensive pizzas in magical surroundings.

4. Osteria Mocenigo

📍M1 🏠 Salizzada San Stae, S Croce 1919 📞 041 523 17 03 · €

Don't miss the *cestino al parmiggiano*, a crisp fried pastry and cheese basket filled with prawns at this traditional Venetian restaurant.

5. Muro

📍N2 🏠 Campiello dello Spezier, Santa Croce 📞 041 524 16 28 · €

Order steak or fish here – Antipasto Muro is a great seafood selection.

6. Antica Birraria La Corte

📍M3 🏠 Campo S Polo, S Polo 2168 🕒 Tue 🌐 birrarialacorte.it · €

Pizzas named after the city's bridges are served at this restaurant set in a former brewery. There is also a tree-shaded patio.

7. Gelateria Polo Nord

📍B3 🏠 Ramo Quinto Gallion O del Pezzetto, S Croce 273 📞 348 033 25 08 🕒 Jan & Dec · €

This artisan *gelateria* serves *Crema Veneziana*, swirled with chocolate and candied orange, and *Budino Goloso*, which has Marsala wine and biscuits.

8. Taverna Da Baffo

📍L3 🏠 Campiello Sant'Agostin, S Polo 2346 🌐 tavernadabaffo.com · €

Seek out this tranquil square for a light lunch with a glass of Belgian beer or crisp Friuli wine.

9. Pasticceria Rizzardini

📍M3 🏠 Campiello dei Meloni, S Polo 1415 🕒 Tue, Aug · €

This old-style pastry shop serves thick hot chocolate and divine fruit tarts, almond slices and peanut toffee.

10. Osteria Bancogiro

📍P2 🏠 Campo S Giacometto, S Polo 122 🕒 Mon 🌐 osteriabancogiro.it · €€

This is a trendy restaurant-bar along the Grand Canal serving a variety of quality Italian vintages and tasty nibbles.

Outdoor seating on the terrace at Osteria Bancogiro

DORSODURO

A district of contrasts, Dorsoduro stretches from the port, via the panoramic Zattere and Grand Canal, all the way to the Punta della Dogana. Highlights for visitors include two foremost art galleries, the Accademia and the Peggy Guggenheim Collection, crammed with masterpieces ancient and modern, as well as Ca' Rezzonico palace and magnificent churches, Santa Maria della Salute and San Sebastiano, the latter famous for its wonderful Veronese works. Literally the "hard backbone" of Venice, built on elevated islands of compacted subsoil, Dorsoduro used to be sparsely populated. Today, as home to most of the city's university premises, it is full of lively cafés, vintage boutiques, bars and nightlife, concentrated in the market square, Campo Santa Margherita. The *bacaris* (cheaper bars) serving *cicchetti* (small snacks) throughout the day are popular.

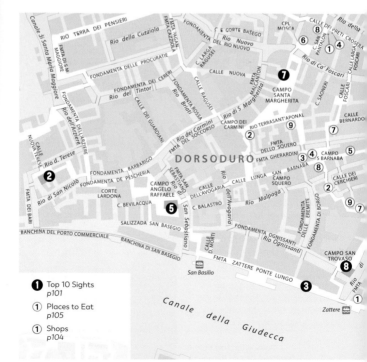

❶ Top 10 Sights
p101

① Places to Eat
p105

① Shops
p104

For places to stay in this area, see p149

1 Accademia Galleries

Housing the largest collection of Venetian art in existence, the Gallerie dell'Accademia (p38) has interactive galleries and ceiling paintings.

2 San Nicolò dei Mendicoli

📍 A5 🏠 Campo S Nicolò, Dorsoduro 1907 🕐 10am–noon & 3–5:30pm Mon–Sat; 9am–noon Sun & hols 🌐 anzolomendicoli.it

This Veneto-Byzantine church with an imposing square campanile (bell tower) is known to film buffs from Nicholas Roeg's horror film *Don't Look Now*. It has a portico that doubled as a shelter for the poor. Founded in the 7th century, it is the second-oldest church in Venice. In the 1970s it was restored by the Venice in Peril Fund, who waterproofed the low floor.

The Zattere waterfront overlooking the Giudecca Canal

3 Zattere

📍 C5

This waterfront took its name from the rafts of timber (*zattere*), which floated downstream from the forests in the northern Dolomite region. The wood was either used for constructing palaces or for shipbuilding. The sailing ships and rowing boats that used to moor here have since been replaced by motorized vaporetti and tourist launches. Today the Zattere offers lovely lagoon views and is perfect for a daytime or evening stroll.

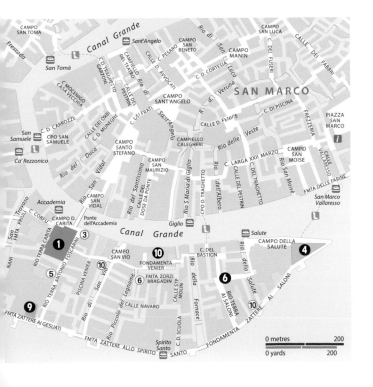

4 Punta della Dogana

📍 E5 🏛 Campo della Salute, Dorsoduro 2 🕐 10am–7pm Wed–Mon 🌐 palazzo grassi.it 🛈

This exciting addition to the Venetian contemporary art scene is housed in an imposing 17th-century customs building, the interior of which was restored by Japanese architect Tadao Ando. It contains important works, including pieces by British artists Rachel Whiteread and the Chapman Brothers, and offers fantastic views towards St Mark's, San Giorgio and the two main canals of Venice. Tickets also grant entry into the Palazzo Grassi (p88).

5 Chiesa di San Sebastiano

📍 B5 🏛 Campo S Sebastiano, Dorsoduro 1907 🕐 10:30am–5pm Mon–Sat 🌐 chorusvenezia.org 🛈

This 16th-century church (p55) is a treasure trove of Paolo Veronese paintings. The artist devoted most of his life to its fresco cycle.

6 Rio Terrà dei Catecumeni

📍 D5

A reclaimed thoroughfare between the Zattere and Santa Maria della Salute, this stretch is dominated by a long building, now a school, where prisoners-of-war of the Republic who did not profess the Christian faith were held captive until they converted. This quiet backwater comes alive on 21 November with the Salute festivities (p81).

7 Campo Santa Margherita

The square of Santa Margherita (p46) is the lively hub of western Dorsoduro. Market stalls, offbeat shops and cafés attract many young people. The colourful fish stalls sell live eels and lobster, the *erborista* aternative medicine, and the bakers some of the tastiest loaves in Venice. The former church of Santa Margherita, now an auditorium owned by the university, lies to the north of the square. Visitors can see sculptural fragments from the original 18th-century church, including gargoyles on the truncated campanile and adjacent house.

8 Squero di San Trovaso

📍 C5

This is the city's most famous gondola repair and construction yard, though

MASKS

Handmade in papier-mâché and glittery plaster, Venetian masks are now strictly tourist fare, but they were once essential attire during Carnival, allowing aristocrats to enjoy themselves in anonymity. One unusual model, with a long curved nose, was used by doctors during plagues, its cavity filled with perfumed herbs to filter the diseased air.

The Punta della Dogana
at dusk

its days may be numbered. The
combined workshop-dwelling
is reminiscent of an Alpine chalet,
as the first occupants came from
the mountainous Cadore region.
Closed to visitors, it backs on to
a canal (Rio di San Trovaso), so it's
easy to watch the caulking and
cleaning in progress.

9 Chiesa dei Gesuati
C5 Fondamente
delle Zattere, Dorsoduro 917
10:30am–5pm Mon–Sat
chorusvenezia.org

Set right on the Zattere waterfront
close to the main ferry moorings,
the Gesuati (also known as Santa
Maria del Rosario) is often confused
with the Gesuiti (Jesuit) establishment in Cannaregio. Taking over
from a minor religious order, the
Domenican friars had this church
constructed in Classical style in
1726 by Giorgio Massari. Inside,
the ceiling consists of three
uplifting frescoes (1737–9) by
Tiepolo, considered among his
best work, portraying St Dominic
amid glorious angels in flight.

10 Peggy Guggenheim Collection

Intended as a four-storey palace,
this building never rose beyond
the ground floor. It was in 1949,
that the building was bought as
a home by Peggy Guggenheim,
a collector, dealer and patron of
the arts. She had her vast collection
of modern European and American
art in this museum (p48) which
was inaugurated in 1980. Today,
the Guggenheim remains among
Venice's most visited sights. The
light-filled rooms and the modern
canvases provide a striking contrast
to the Renaissance paintings which
are the main attraction in Venetian
churches and museums.

EXPLORING DORSODURO

Morning
The **Accademia Galleries** (p38)
are vast, so focus your visit on a
selection of its masterpieces, but
don't neglect the Carpaccios and
Bellinis. After all that art, have a
coffee watching the boats go by
at **Snack Bar Accademia
Foscarini** (*Rio Terrà Antonio
Foscarini, Dorsoduro 878/C; 041
522 72 81*), a magical spot right at
the foot of Accademia Bridge.

Next, head off east for a stroll,
past Longhena's work of art, the
church of **Santa Maria della
Salute** (p35), to **Punta della
Dogana**, a great spot for taking
photos of Piazza San Marco. Turn
back in the direction of the
Zattere (p101) and Giudecca
Canal. **Al Chioschetto** (*Zattere,
Dorsoduro 1406/A; closed Dec–mid-
Jan*), a bar right on the water's
edge, is a good spot for lunch.

Afternoon
Wander through to **Campo Santa
Margherita** to the **Scuola Grande
dei Carmini** (p47) to admire
Tiepolo's canvases, then take
some time to admire the architectural curiosities of this square.

As sunset approaches, grab a table
for a Spritz aperitivo at the trendy
bar **Margaret DuChamp** (*Campo
S Margherita, Dorsoduro 3019; 041
528 62 55*). It's a good place for
people-watching, and an added
bonus is the scent of jasmine that
fills the air as night falls.

Shops

1. 3856
📍 K4 🏠 Calle San Pantalon, Dorsoduro 3749 🕒 Sun

A curated selection of clothing and accessories is available at this shop run by a mother-daughter team.

2. Libreria Marco Polo
📍 B4 🏠 Campo Santa Margherita, Dorsoduro 2899 🌐 libreriamarco polo.com

An independent bookshop, Libreria Marco Polo has new and secondhand books in Italian, English, French and German. Local poetry readings and book presentations are hosted here.

3. Totem-Il Canale Gallery
📍 C5 🏠 Rio Terrà Antonio Foscarini, Dorsoduro 878/B 🕒 Tue

Bulky ancient beads, made with vitreous paste and once traded in Africa, count as precious antiques. There are modern African wood artworks too.

4. Signor Blum
📍 K5 🏠 Campo S Barnaba, Dorsoduro 2840 🌐 signorblum.it

Detailed jigsaw models of Gothic palaces, flanked by wall panels and painted toy figures are handmade by this co-operative of female artisans.

5. Augusto Mazzon
📍 L5 🏠 Calle del Traghetto, Dorsoduro 2783

Everyone's Christmas tree needs one of the joyous gilded cherubs lovingly

A wood-carving workshop at Augusto Mazzon

crafted by wood-carver and painter Danilo. He also makes picture frames and furniture.

6. Officina Veneziana
📍 K4 🏠 Campo S Pantalon, Dorsoduro 3701 🕒 Sun

Choose from a wonderful selection of Art Deco jewellery, Easter eggs, Christmas decorations and fine china.

7. Perla Madre Design
📍 K5 🏠 Calle del Fabbro, Dorsoduro 3182 🕒 Sun 🌐 perlamadredesign.com

Colourful glass bead jewellery is made right in front of your eyes by designer Simona Iacovazzi.

8. Madera
📍 K5 🏠 Campo S Barnaba, Dorsoduro 2762 🕒 Sun 🌐 maderavenezia.it

This contemporary design store has minimalist pieces in wood and glass, as well as gorgeous ceramics.

9. Libreria Toletta
📍 L6 🏠 Sacca della Toletta, Dorsoduro 1213 🌐 latoletta.com

Specializing in art and architecture, this popular bookshop also has a great collection of guidebooks and novels in English.

10. Marisa Convento at Bottega Cini
📍 C6 🏠 Dorsoduro 862 🕒 Tue & Wed 🌐 marisaconvento.it

Marisa Convento creates jewels with coral branches using unique Murano small beads at this concept store.

Handmade toy figures at Signor Blum

Places to Eat

1. Gelateria Nico
C5 **Fondamenta Zattere, Dorsoduro 922** Thu & early Nov–early Feb **gelaterianico.com · €**

This spot is Venice's most renowned ice-cream parlour. *Gianduiotto da passeggio* – hazelnut and chocolate ice cream smothered in whipped cream – is a local favourite.

2. Osteria Enoteca Ai Artisti
C5 **Fondamenta della Toletta, Dorsoduro 1169/A** Sun & Mon, mid-Aug & late Dec–early Jan **enotecaartisti.com · €€**

Try the seafood ravioli at this welcoming canal-side restaurant.

3. La Bitta
K6 **Calle Lunga de San Barnaba, Dorsoduro 2753** 041 523 05 31 Dec · €€

Fine Italian wines accompany a superb menu at this restaurant. Leave room for one of their delicious desserts.

4. Impronta Caffè
K4 **Calle dei Preti, Dorsoduro 3815** Sun **improntarestaurantvenice.com · €**

Affordable meals and long opening hours make this a local favourite.

5. La Rivista
C5 **Rio Terrà Foscarini, Dorsoduro 979/A** Mon & Sun pm **capisanihotel.it · €€**

Innovative Italian cuisine is offered here, in relaxing, designer surroundings. There is an inspiring choice of cold platters of cheese and meats. The wine list is impressive.

6. Ai Gondolieri
D5 **Ponte del Formager, Dorsoduro 366** Tue **aigondolieri.it · €€**

One of the city's top restaurants, Ai Gondolieri specializes in game from the Veneto when in season.

7. Bar alla Toletta
L6 **Dorsoduro 1191 · €**

This bar is renowned for its fresh sandwiches, which are generously filled.

8. Pasticceria Tonolo
K4 **Crosera S Pantalon, Dorsoduro 3764** Mon & Sun pm **pasticceria-tonolo-venezia.business.site · €**

Try freshly baked almond biscuits and mini pizzas at this famous pastry shop.

9. Gelateria Il Doge
K5 **Campo S Margherita, Dorsoduro 3058/A** 041 523 46 07 Dec & Jan · €

Treat yourself to the *Crema del Doge* (candied fruit, egg custard and chocolate) at this great ice-cream parlour.

10. Linea d'Ombra
D5 **Ponte dell'Umiltà, Dorsoduro** Wed, early Jan–Feb & mid-Nov–Dec **ristorante lineadombra.com · €€€**

Enjoy the waterside setting behind the landmark Salute church. Specialities on the menu include tuna tartare and sea bass in a salt crust.

The lovely waterside terrace at Linea d'Ombra

CANNAREGIO

Accounting for the huge crescent between the northern bank of the Grand Canal and the lagoon, the bustling area of Cannaregio reaches from the railway station to the city hospital. It was home to Marco Polo and artists Titian and Tintoretto, and it features landmark churches such as Madonna dell'Orto along with the old Jewish Ghetto. Named after the *canne* (reeds) that once filled its marshes, it is crossed by Strada Nova, the city's main thoroughfare, but also contains Venice's narrowest alley, the 58-cm- (23-inch-) wide Calle Varisco. This vibrant area has its own market, craft workshops and rowing clubs, while relaxation comes at the string of shady parks and laid-back cafés and bars that line the maze of backstreet canals.

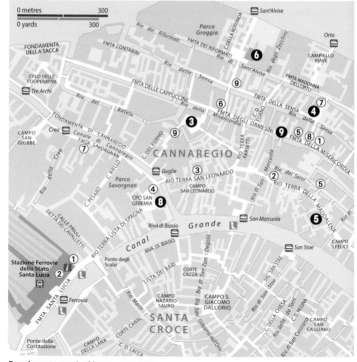

For places to stay in this area, see p150

Walking over a footbridge to the Santa Maria dei Miracoli

1 Santa Maria dei Miracoli

📍 Q2 🏛 Campo dei Miracoli, Cannaregio 🕐 10:30am–5pm Mon–Sat 🌐 chorusvenezia.org ♿

A "jewellery box" of marble slabs and exquisite bas-reliefs, this Renaissance church (*p55*) was named after a miracle-working icon from 1409, said to have resuscitated a drowned man and now enshrined in the main altar.

2 Corte Seconda del Milion

📍 Q2

The restructured Malibran Theatre, situated in this square, was erected in the 1790s on the site of a house, where the explorer Marco Polo (*p56*) was born. Other early Gothic buildings remain, their timber overhangs set off by bright-red geraniums. Along with the adjoining bridge, the square was named after the explorer whose stories about the East in *Il Milione* continue to inspire travellers.

3 Jewish Ghetto

📍 C1 🏛 Museo Ebraico, Campo del Ghetto Nuovo, Cannaregio 2902/B 🕐 10am–5:30pm Sun–Fri (last adm: 4pm) 🚫 Public & Jewish hols 🌐 museoebraico.it ♿

The word "ghetto" originated in Venice, derived from *getto* (casting) due to an old iron foundry here. By 1492, many Jewish refugees reached Venice after expulsion from Spain, and in 1516, were obliged by law to move to this area. Their movements around Venice were restricted; they were subject to a curfew and forced to sleep behind locked gates. Waves of arrivals saw each language group build its own synagogue and raise the buildings in height. Today, the city has a thriving Jewish community, but few still live in the ghetto. The synagogues can be visited with a guide; don't miss the Museo Ebraico (museum of sacred objects).

JEWISH PEOPLE IN VENICE

Banned by Republic law from practising manual trades, many Jewish people were skilled doctors or moneylenders. Most were refugees from other parts of Europe, and they left a cultural legacy, including music, dance and the Venetian language. As remembered by a memorial in the former ghetto, few returned from the Nazi camps of World War II.

[Map of Cannaregio area showing: Canale delle Fondamente Nuove, Sacca della Misericordia, CORTE VECCHIA, Rio di Noale, C. DELLA RACCHETTA, Rio della Racchetta, Rio di San Felice, C. L. SANTA CATERINA, FONDAMENTA NUOVE, C. MARCO FOSCARINI, CAMPO DEI GESUITI, Fondamenta Nuove, Rio di Cà Dolce, Rio dei Gesuiti, CORTE CARITA, CALLE DEL FUMO, RIO TERRA D. S. APOSTOLI, STRADA NOVA, Ca' d'Oro, CAMPIELLO WIDMAN, CAMPO DEI S. APOSTOLI, Rio di Santi Apostoli, SAL. S. CANCIANO, RUGA D. SPEZIALI, CAMPO D. PESCHERIA, Rialto Mercato, CAMPO SAN MARINA — with markers 6, 7, 8, 10, 3, 4, 1, 2]

Beautiful ceiling frescoe at the Chiesa di Sant'Alvise

4 Campo dei Mori
📍 D1

In this odd, funnel-shaped square, your attention is drawn to three statues of Arabian-style "Moors" – but neither North African nor Muslim, they hailed from Morea in Greece. Rioba, Sandi and Afani Mastelli were medieval traders who made their home in the family palace around the corner. Next to the bridge over Rio della Sensa is a doorway marked No 3399, once the home of renowned 16th-century artist Tintoretto *(p60)*.

5 Farmacia Ponci
📍 D2 🏠 Strada Nova, Cannaregio 2233/A 🕐 Sat pm & Sun

The "Casa degli Speziali", the oldest pharmacy in Venice, carries on its business in modern premises alongside its restored 16th-century rooms. Displayed on original briarwood, shelving adorned with Baroque statues in Arolla pinewood, are rows of 17th-century porcelain jars used for storing medicinal ingredients; for safety reasons, poisons were kept in a rear room. Pharmacies were strictly regulated and numbered 518 in 1564, the year their guild was formed.

6 Chiesa di Sant'Alvise
📍 C1 🏠 Campo S Alvise, Cannaregio 🕐 10:30am–5pm Mon–Sat 🌐 chorusvenezia.org 🔗

This church is said to have been commissioned by a Venetian noblewoman in 1388 to honour Saint Louis of Toulouse after the saint appeared to her in a dream. Major restoration took place in the 17th century, when the ceiling was painted with frescoes by Pietro Antonio Torri and Pietro Ricchi. Other notable works of art in the church include paintings by Giambattista Tiepolo – *Ascent to Calvary*, *Crowning with Thorns* and *The Flagellation*.

7 Ca' d'Oro
📍 N1 🏠 Calle Ca' d'Oro, Cannaregio 3932 🕐 10am–7pm Tue–Sun (last adm: 6:30pm) 🕐 1 Jan, 1 May & 25 Dec 🌐 cadoro.org 🔗

Behind the resplendent "golden palace" of Ca' D'Oro's Gothic tracery is a column-filled courtyard paved with coloured tesserae. Inside is the Galleria Giorgio Franchetti, a collection of paintings, sculptures and ceramics donated to the State by Baron Giorgio Franchetti in 1916, along with the building. One highlight is Andrea Mantegna's painting *St Sebastian* (1560) pierced by arrows "like a hedgehog", in the portico leading to a loggia overlooking the Grand Canal. An ornate 15th-century staircase leads to 16th-century Flemish tapestries on the second floor.

8 Palazzo Labia

C2 🏛 Campo S Geremia, Cannaregio 🚫 To the public

Abandoned when its wealthy merchant owners fled to Vienna at the fall of the Republic, this 17th-century palace overlooking the Canal di Cannaregio acted as a silk factory, saw-mill and primary school, but was badly damaged in 1945 when a boat loaded with munitions blew up in front of it. Luckily, the wonderful ballroom frescoed by Tiepolo has been restored. The palace belongs to RAI, the state broadcasting service.

9 Fondamente della Misericordia and degli Ormesini

C2

Parallel to the Strada Nova but worlds away from the tourist bustle, these adjoining quaysides have a real neighbourhood feel. There's a good sprinkling of *osterie* (wine bars) alongside coffee houses and bookshops. The area is enjoying a renaissance of sorts and foodies will be spoilt for choice. The word *"ormesini"* derives from a rich fabric traded through Hormuz, now in Iran, and imitated in Florence and Venice. Ormesini leads into Misericordia and to the towering red-brick Scuola Grande building. Used as the city's basketball team headquarters for many years, it occasionally opens for temporary exhibitions.

10 Fondamente Nuove

E2

Opposite the cemetery island of San Michele *(p119)*, this lagoon-side pavement is an important jumping-off point for ferries to the northern islands and sports one of the city's rare petrol stations. The ample quaysides were not constructed and paved until the mid-1500s; until then the waterfront reached back to Titian's garden (No 5113, Calle Larga dei Botteri), giving unobstructed views of the Alps on a clear day.

Ca' d'Oro's intricately carved arches overlooking the Grand Canal

EXPLORING CANNAREGIO

Morning

Begin the day with the Galleria Franchetti in the lovely **Ca d'Oro** *(p108)*, but leave plenty of time to explore the rest of the palace, making sure that you take in the balconies overlooking the Grand Canal and the mosaics in the courtyard. Afterwards, head to **Torrefazione Cannaregio** *(p73)* for a cup of the best coffee in town. Only minutes away is the fascinating **Jewish Ghetto** *(p107)*, where you can take an informative guided tour of the many remaining synagogues in the area.

For a change from pasta and pizza, try **Orient Experience** *(Rio Terà Farsetti, Fondamenta di Cannaregio, Cannaregio 1847)* for lunch.

Afternoon

Wander up the canal towards the unusual, three-arched **Ponte dei Tre Archi** *(p65)*. Return over the bridge and head for **Fondamenta della Sacca**, which affords good views of the Dolomites on a clear day. Many ways lead east from here, but try to take in the church of **Madonna dell'Orto** *(p55)* for the Tintoretto paintings, then **Campo dei Mori** to see the house where the artist once lived.

On Fondamenta Ormesini, pop into **Al Timon** *(Fondamenta Ormesini, Cannaregio 2754)*, where energetic waiters will serve you north Italian wine.

Specialist Shops

1. Boutique Lègami
📍 B2 🏠 Fondamenta S Lucia 20, Cannaregio 🌐 legami.com

This popular Italian brand offers stationery items and accessories featuring home, leisure and travel, as well as excellent gift items.

2. Mori & Bozzi
📍 D2 🏠 Rio Terrà della Maddalena, Cannaregio 2367

One of the best shoe shops in Venice offers an irresistible selection of women's footwear, clothes and accessories.

3. San Leonardo Market
📍 C2 🏠 Rio Terrà San Leonardo 🕐 Sun

In the morning and late afternoon this area functions as a lively open-air produce market. In autumn the air is thick with the aroma of roasting chestnuts.

4. Luna Darin
📍 C2 🏠 Salizzada S Geremia, Cannaregio 316

Come here for handmade glass beads in brilliant hues and shapes, window hangings and Christmas decorations.

5. Costumi Nicolao Atelier
📍 C1 🏠 Fondamenta dei Ormesini, Cannaregio 2590 🕐 Sat & Sun

This is the place to go to hire a Carnival outfit. It offers a wide range of period costumes and formal evening wear. It also organizes mask-making courses.

6. Codex
📍 C2 🏠 Fondamenta Ormesini, Cannaregio 2778

This studio and exhibition space of resident artists Nelson Kishi and Robin Frood sells original drawings, paintings, prints and posters.

7. Momylia
📍 D2 🏠 Calle dei Mori 3378, Cannaregio 🕐 Sun

Producing handmade Murano glass beads and jewellery, this small shop also has a laboratory where brief demonstrations are held.

8. Salmoiraghi & Viganò
📍 D2 🏠 Strada Nova, Cannaregio 3928–3930

Italian spectacles are stylish and good value, and this well-reputed optometrist can make up prescription glasses the same day.

9. Arte Ebraica Shalom
📍 C1 🏠 Ghetto Vecchio, Cannaregio 1218 🕐 Sat & Jewish hols

An artisan shop that specializes in Jewish handicrafts such as menorahs made with Murano glass or bronze, and mezuzahs with mosaic designs.

10. Gianni Basso
📍 E2 🏠 Calle del Fumo, Cannaregio 5306 🕐 Sat pm & Sun

The handmade stationery on offer at this shop is made by a modest artisan and is popular with international VIPs.

Bustling market stalls at the San Leonardo market

Places to Eat

1. Il Paradiso Perduto

📍 D2 🏠 Fondamenta della Misericordia 2540, Cannareggio 🕙 Tue, Wed & Thu am 🌐 ilparadiso perduto.wordpress.com · €

An *osteria* with a menu that changes daily. Try *il gran fritoin*, a fried fish made with white polenta.

2. Grom

📍 B3 🏠 Fondamenta S Lucia, Cannaregio 1 🌐 grom.it/en · €

Ice creams, sorbets, milkshakes and more are served at this Italian gelato chain.

3. Ostaria Boccadoro

📍 E3 🏠 Campo Widman, Cannaregio 5405 🕙 Mon & Dec–Mar 🌐 boccadorovenezia.it · €€€

Pasta dishes and blends of seafood and seasonal vegetables are on offer here, as well as an extensive wine list.

4. Taverna del Campiello Remer

📍 D3 🏠 Campiello Remer, Cannaregio 5701 🌐 tavernaremer.com · €€€

A converted warehouse with upturned barrels as tables. It offers a buffet.

5. Il Santo Bevitore

📍 D2 🏠 Campo S Fosca, Cannaregio 2393 🌐 ilsantobevitorepub.com · €

Enjoy a range of quality beers and snacks at this laid-back bar with live music.

6. Vini da Gigio

📍 D2 🏠 Fondamenta S Felice, Cannaregio 3628/A 🕙 Mon & Tue, 2 weeks in Jan & Aug 🌐 vinida gigio.com · €€

Canal-side restaurant serving innovative traditional dishes.

Grom, known for its gelato and milkshake

7. Al Parlamento

📍 B2 🏠 Fondamenta Savorgnan, Cannaregio 511 🌐 alparlamento.it · €

Appetizing, simple meals are served at this café set beside the canal.

8. Da Rioba

📍 D2 🏠 Fondamenta Misericordia, Cannaregio 2553 🕙 Mon 🌐 darioba.com · €€–€€€

The impeccably presented Venetian fish-based dishes on the menu at this restaurant are given a tasteful modern twist.

9. Osteria Anice Stellato

📍 C1 🏠 Fondamenta della Sensa, Cannaregio 3272 🕙 Mon & Sun, 2 weeks in Aug 🌐 osteria nicestellato.com · €€

It is important to book well ahead for this popular place. Among the culinary delights on offer are fish and meat dishes, as well as a wonderful *zabaglione* dessert.

10. La Bottega Ai Promessi Sposi

📍 P1 🏠 Calle dell'Oca, Cannaregio 4367 📞 041 241 27 47 🕙 Mon L · €

This low-key restaurant offers diners tasty *cicchetti* (bar snacks) while friendly staff serve more substantial traditional Venetian fare, including vegetarian options.

CASTELLO

Named after a castle possibly built here in Roman times, Castello is the "fishtail" of Venice. The western half of the district houses historic highlights such as the churches of Santi Giovanni e Paolo and San Zaccaria. However, half of Castello is taken up with shipbuilding, focusing on the historic Arsenale. The Giardini is the venue for the Biennale art exhibition.

1 Chiesa di San Francesco della Vigna

F3 🏠 Campo S Francesco della Vigna, Castello 2786 **📞** 041 522 24 76 **🕐** Apr–Oct: 10am–4pm daily; Nov–Mar: 10am–noon & 2–4pm daily

In the back alleys of Castello, this Franciscan church sports a combination of architectural styles courtesy of both Sansovino and Palladio (p61), who designed the façade. The church was originally built on the site of a small chapel in a vineyard, which was donated by the aristocrat Marco Ziani. The colonnaded cloister can be seen while you're admiring Giovanni Bellini's *Madonna and Child* (1507). Another highlight is Veronese's *Virgin and Child with Saints* (1551). Playgrounds have replaced the 13th-century *vigna* (vineyard).

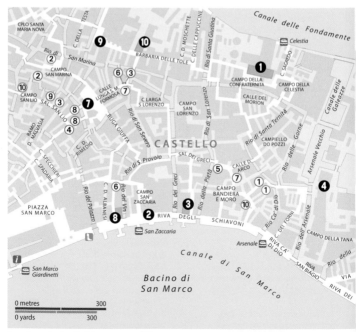

For places to stay in this area, see p150

Gondolas moored along the Riva degli Schiavoni

2 Riva degli Schiavoni
⑨ F4

Thronging with tour groups and packed with souvenir stalls, this quayside affords a lovely promenade past majestic palaces (now mostly hotels) and a much photographed 1887 monument to the first king of Italy, Vittorio Emanuele. It is linked to Piazza San Marco by the elegant Istrian stone bridge Ponte della Paglia, named after the *paglia* (straw) once unloaded from barges here. This is also the best place for taking pictures of the Bridge of Sighs. At the eastern end is the Ca' di Dio ("house of God"), a 13th-century hospice for pilgrims en route to the Holy Land.

3 Santa Maria della Pietà
⑨ F4 🏠 Riva degli Schiavoni, Castello 3701 ⏰ 10:30am–1pm & 2:30–5:50pm daily 🌐 pietavenezia.org ↗

Inextricably linked with the composer and musician Antonio Vivaldi, this Classical-fronted church designed by Giorgio Massari belonged to the adjoining home for foundlings where he taught. It is best seen by attending an evening concert to appreciate Tiepolo's ceiling fresco, exalting music and the young choristers, identifiable by the sprigs of pomegranate blossom they wear. The choir stalls accommodated both the singers and the nobility, who were not expected to mix with the commoners.

4 Arsenale
⑨ G3 🏠 Castello

Aptly named after the Arab word *darsina'a* ("house of industry"), Venice's Arsenale shipyards at their peak employed an army of 16,000 to produce the fleets that sailed the Mediterranean, spreading and protecting the influence of the Republic through trade deals and naval superiority. With its innovative assembly-line system, the Arsenale could construct a galley in a few hours, notably in 1574 while the French king Henry III enjoyed a banquet. The stone lions that guard the entrance hail from Greek islands and were looted by Venetian commanders.

Nuove

ARSENALE

Dársena Grande

FONDAMENTA ARSENALE

Rio de San Gerolamo

S. STRETTA

Canale di San Pietro

CAMPO SAN PIETRO

CAMPO DI RUGA

⑤

Il Tana

Rio di Sant'Anna

⑥ G. GARIBALDI **⑨**

VIALE GIUSEPPE GARIBALDI

CALLE ANCORE

CALLE CORERA

SECO MARINA

④

SETTE MARTIRI

⑤

5 San Pietro di Castello

🅟 H4 🏛 Chiesa di San Pietro di Castello ⏰ 10:30am–5pm 🌐 chorusvenezia.org

Venice's religious headquarters were here until 1807, when the Basilica di San Marco became the city's cathedral. Linked to the rest of Castello by two broad bridges, San Pietro attracts artists for its evocative, forlorn air, and fun-lovers for the late-June neighbourhood fair. Art lovers come for the church with works by Veronese and Coducci.

6 Via Garibaldi and Giardini

🅟 H5

A pleasant avenue lined with cafés and a market, Via Garibaldi was named when the eponymous general marched into Venice in 1866 as part of his campaign for Unification. Take a stroll to the Giardini (public gardens). To make way for the park in 1807, architect Selva *(p61)* demolished four churches and convents and a sailors' hospice.

7 Campo Santa Maria Formosa

🅟 E3 🏛 Chiesa di Santa Maria Formosa ⏰ 10:30am–5pm Mon–Sat 🌐 chorusvenezia.org 🗺

A lovely rounded church on this sun-blessed square appears to spread in all directions, the result of a 7th-century bishop's vision of the *formosa* ("shapely") Virgin Mary's request that it be built where "a white cloud came to rest". Artworks are by Vivarini and Palma il Vecchio. The square is a good place for a picnic or a game of football, in lieu of the bullfights and re-enactments of Venice's conquests held here in the olden days.

8 Hotel Danieli

This enchanting 15th-century palace with a pink Gothic façade is set on the magnificent waterfront near Piazza San Marco. After a string of aristocratic proprietors, it was taken over in 1822 by Joseph da Niel, who turned it into a hotel with an illustrious guest list, including Dickens, Wagner and Ruskin. In the 1940s an annexe was added amid great

---

THE VENICE BIENNALE

The Giardini and its beautiful tree-lined avenues were inaugurated as an international exhibition area in 1895 under the entrepreneur Count Volpi di Misurata. Every two years, more than 50 countries send artists to represent them, each with their own pavilion custom-designed by some of the world's leading architects, such as Alvar Aalto, Carlo Scarpa and James Stirling.

Tree-lined Giardini, one of Venice's best-known public parks

Distinct Gothic façade of Hotel Danieli, on the waterfront

controversy – since 1102 no dwelling over one floor had been allowed on the site. The redeeming feature of the 1940s wing is the roof restaurant.

9 Campo Santi Giovanni e Paolo

🗺 E3

Dominated by the brick façade of the Gothic church SS Giovanni e Paolo, this square welcomes visitors with a flotilla of outdoor cafés. Worthy of contemplation is one of the world's most magnificent equestrian statues, a stylized 15th-century portrait of the great *condottiere* (mercenary leader) Bartolomeo Colleoni. He left a legacy to the city on the condition that his statue be erected in front of San Marco, craftily "interpreted" by the governors as the nearby Scuola Grande di San Marco. Decorated with arches and trompe l'oeil panels by Lombard masters, this former confraternity serves as the public hospital.

10 Ospedaletto

🗺 F3 🏛 Barbaria delle Tole, Castello 6691 🕐 Mar-Oct: 10am–6pm daily; Nov–Feb: 9:30am–5:30pm daily 🔗

The sculptures on the façade of this almshouse church, built by Andrea Palladio in 1575, were added by Baldassare Longhena in 1674. Pass through the church to the Sala della Musica, where female wards of the orphanage once gave concerts.

A DAY IN CASTELLO

Morning

After a visit to the Gothic church on **Campo Santi Giovanni e Paolo**, visit the city's hospital. Although it is now ultra-modern inside, you can still appreciate the Renaissance façade, and a series of ancient courtyards and confraternity buildings. Have a coffee and cake at the old-style **Rosa Salva** (*Campo SS Giovanni e Paolo, Castello 6779*).

Take a stroll, via **Campo Santa Maria Formosa**, to Campo San Zaccaria and the church with its Bellini painting, and **Scuola di San Giorgio degli Schiavoni** (*p63*) for its Carpaccio works. For lunch, **Via Garibaldi** is a good bet, at one of the cafés or at **Il Nuovo Galeon** (*Via Giuseppe Garibaldi 1309*).

Afternoon

Head east along **Via Garibaldi**, and detour briefly into the shady avenue for the statue of Giuseppe Garibaldi and his followers. After a visit to the island of **San Pietro di Castello**, go back via the lagoon and the **Giardini**. A poignant sculpture to the female partisans of World War II can be seen at water level.

Continue in the direction of San Marco, just past the mouth of Via Garibaldi. On the embankment is **Angiò Bar** (*Riva di S Biasio, Castello 2142; closed Tue*), the perfect spot for a Venetian sunset with wine and snacks.

Browsing books at the Libreria Acqua Alta

Specialist Shops

1. Le Ceramiche
📍 F4 🏠 Calle del Pestrin, Castello 3876 🕐 Wed & Thu

Alessandro Merlin crafts original plates and tiles with black and white designs based on lagoon fish or human figures in this atelier close to the Arsenale (*p113*).

2. VizioVirtù Cioccolateria
📍 E3 🏠 Calle Forneri, Castello 5988 🌐 viziovirtu.com

This factory creates chocolates from traditional Venetian recipes. Specialities include spiced hot chocolate and pralines. Book a tasting tour in advance.

3. Papier Mâché
📍 R3 🏠 Calle Lunga Santa Maria Formosa, Castello 5174

This is one of the few traditional mask shops in town. It also sells beautiful ceramics.

4. Manufactus Venezia
📍 E4 🏠 Calle delle Bande, Castello 5275 🌐 manufactus.it

A traditional bookbindery where you can also find leather bags and accessories designed and made in Italy.

5. Il Ponte dei Sogni
📍 F4 🏠 Salita Sant'Antonin, Castello 3473 🕐 Sun

Filled with Venice-themed gifts for both children and adults, most of the items here are handmade by the shop owner.

6. Libreria Acqua Alta
📍 R3 🏠 Calle Lunga Santa Maria Formosa, Castello 5176

With ancient volumes piled high and Venetian-specific literature, Libreria Acqua Alta is a fascinating bookshop that has a gondola full of books inside.

7. Muranero
📍 F4 🏠 Salizzada del Pignater, Castello 3545 🕐 Sun–Tue 🌐 collectionmuranero.art

Senegalese artist Niang Moulaye creates beautiful handmade jewellery, combining African style with Murano glass bead-making techniques.

8. Ratti
📍 F4 🏠 Calle del Pistor, Castello 5979 🕐 Sat pm & Sun 🌐 rattivenezia.com

This shop sells household items such as the quintessential Italian coffee pot, along with mobile phones and hardware.

9. Corte delle Fate
📍 E3 🏠 Salizzada S Lio, Castello 5690

Modern footwear and quirky accessories are available here in the shape of bags, jewellery and on-trend clothing.

10. Giovanna Zanella
📍 Q3 🏠 Calle Carminati, Castello 5641 🕐 Sun & am 🌐 giovannazanella.com

A must for all serious shoppers, this store offers quirky handmade shoes in a fabulous range of incredible designs.

Places to Eat

1. Corte Sconta
⚐ F4 ⌂ Calle del Pestrin, Castello 3886 ⌚ Sun & Mon, Jan, mid-Jul–mid-Aug ⓦ cortescontave.com · €€€

One of Venice's finest restaurants, Corte Sconta is known for its delicious seafood antipasti. Book in advance.

2. Osteria Santa Marina
⚐ Q2 ⌂ Campo S Marina, Castello 5911 ⌚ Sun; Mon lunch, 2 weeks in Jan ⓦ osteriadisantamarina.com · €€€

Sample creative versions of Venetian and Italian fare at this well-reputed restaurant. In summer, diners can enjoy candelight dining outside.

3. Gelateria Gallonetto
⚐ E3 ⌂ Salizzada S Lio, Castello 6727 ☏ 041 847 69 76 ⌚ Jan & Dec · €

Enjoy creamy, delicious ice cream made with fresh products here. The fruit-rich sorbets, the Grand Crus dark chocolate and the fresh mascarpone cream are all excellent.

4. Trattoria dai Tosi Piccoli
⚐ H5 ⌂ Secco Marina, Castello 736–738 ☏ 041 523 71 02 ⌚ Wed & 25 Dec · €

This cheery restaurant is especially popular during the Biennale art exhibition (p114), as it's only a short walk from where all the action takes place. Mouthwatering *pasta della casa* (house pasta) includes seafood and vegetables. There is a pizza menu at dinner.

Diners at Caffè La Serra, a former 19th-century glasshouse

5. Caffè La Serra
⚐ H5 ⌂ Viale Giuseppe Garibaldi, Castello 1254 ⓦ serradeigiardini. org/it · €

Housed in a former greenhouse, La Serra is perfect for a light snack after exploring the gardens of the Biennale.

6. Alla Rivetta
⚐ E4 ⌂ Ponte S Provolo, Castello 4625 ⌚ Mon ⓦ allarivetta.it · €€

This friendly joint has good seafood options and regional dishes.

7. Alla Mascareta
⚐ E3 ⌂ Calle Lunga S Maria Formosa, Castello 5183 ⌚ L · €

A great bar for wine lovers, Alla Mascareta serves antipasti and main dishes.

8. Alle Testiere
⚐ E3 ⌂ Calle del Mondo Nuovo, Castello 5801 ⌚ Sun, Mon, Aug & 23 Dec–10 Jan ⓦ osterialletestiere.it · €€€

There is an unusual selection of fish, cheese and wines here.

9. Nevodi Pizza Lab
⚐ G4 ⌂ Via Giuseppe Garibaldi, Castello 1342 ☏ 045 238 173 ⌚ Mon & Dec–Feb · €

This takeaway pizzeria has an excellent *mozzarella in carrozza* (fried cheese sandwich) and aubergine parmigiana.

10. Al Covo
⚐ F4 ⌂ Campiello de la Pescaria, Castello 3968 ⌚ Tue & Wed, 1 week Aug, 4 weeks Dec–Jan ⓦ ristorante alcovo.com · €€€

Pair sophisticated fish dishes with a choice from the Italian wine list here.

THE NORTHERN LAGOON

The northern lagoon is dotted with mudflats and abandoned islands where rambling monasteries lie crumbling in the sun, backed by sweeping views of snow-capped mountains. Refugees from the mainland, fleeing the Huns, first settled on Torcello, which grew with the additional influx of influential religious orders. Many of the islands became sites for churches, hospitals, powder factories and salt production. Today, however, only a handful of them are still inhabited – glassmaking Murano is the most important, while Burano, Sant'Erasmo and Mazzorbo have sparse populations of fishers and market gardeners.

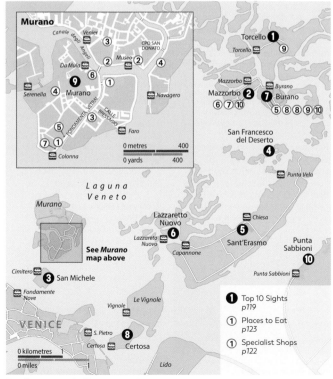

Murano

Canale degli Angeli · Venier ③
CPO SAN DONATO
Da Mula ② Museo ② ④
⑨ Murano ④ ① ⑥
Serenella
Navagero
FONDAMENTA VETRAI · CALLE BRESSAGIO
③
⑤ Faro
⑦ ①
Colonna

0 metres 400
0 yards 400

Torcello ①
Torcello ⑨
Mazzorbo Burano
Mazzorbo ② ⑦ Burano
⑥⑦⑩ ⑤⑧⑧⑨⑩

San Francesco del Deserto ④

Punta Vela

Laguna Veneto

Murano

See *Murano* map above

Lazzaretto Nuovo
Chiesa
Lazzaretto Nuovo ⑥
Capannone ⑤ Sant'Erasmo
Punta Sabbioni ⑩
Punta Sabbioni

Cimitero ③ San Michele
Fondamente Nove

VENICE
Vignole Le Vignole
S. Pietro ⑧
Certosa Certosa
Lido

0 kilometres 1
0 miles 1

① Top 10 Sights p119
① Places to Eat p123
① Specialist Shops p122

For places to stay in this area, see p150

1 Torcello
☑ H1

This lush island (*p44*), a short ferry ride away from Cannaregio, is a welcome escape from the bustle of the city. Established during the 5th and 6th centuries, once-thriving Torcello marks the site of Venice's original settlement – although a visit today makes for a more restful affair.

2 Mazzorbo
☑ H1

This pretty, verdant island exudes a tranquil air as locals tend their vineyards or artichoke fields. Wicker cages for fattening up *moleche* (soft-shelled crabs) hang over the water, and this delicacy can be sampled in the island's trattorias. Amid the scattering of houses are modern council blocks, which are painted in pastel hues. Mazzorbo has its own boat stop but is also joined to Burano by a long timber footbridge.

3 San Michele
☑ G2 ☑ Cemetery: 7:30am–6pm daily (Oct–Mar: to 4:30pm)

San Michele became the city cemetery in 1826, in the wake of a Napoleonic decree that the dead should be buried far from city dwellings to improve hygiene standards. Entry to the cemetery is via a Gothic portal surmounted by St Michael at odds with a dragon. Don't neglect to visit the pretty marble-façaded church next door, designed by Mauro Coducci (*p61*) in 1469. On All Souls' Day (2 November), the island is crowded with relatives paying a visit to their dear departed. However, unless you're a famous resident like Ezra Pound, Igor Stravinsky or Sergei Diaghilev, your remains are dug up after 10 years and placed in an urn to make room for someone else.

4 San Francesco del Deserto
☑ H1 ☑ Monastery: 9–11am & 3–5pm Tue–Sun ☑ sanfrancesco deldeserto.it ☑

Lying just south of the island from Burano, this attractive island of

Aerial view of the San Francesco del Deserto complex

cypress trees is home to a Franciscan monastery. According to legend it was founded by St Francis in person, on his way back from preaching missions in Egypt and Palestine in 1220. Today, the multilingual monks offer informative tours of the monastery and the pristine gardens. In May, clad in their brown habits and sandals, the monks attend the Vogalonga regatta (*p81*) in their heavy duty boat, much to the delight of the Venetian crowds.

5 Sant'Erasmo
☑ H2

Just over 4 km (2.5 miles) long and 1 km (0.5 miles) wide at the broadest point, Sant'Erasmo offers serene countryside, praised enthusiastically by the Romans who built sumptuous villas here. A couple of rickety old motorcars occasionally bump along the lanes, but bicycles and boats are still the main form of transport. The main activities here are market gardening, particularly the production of delicious asparagus and artichokes, which prosper on the sandy soil and are a mainstay of Rialto Market (*p43*). You will also find a small stretch of sandy beach here, too. On the first Sunday in October, a harvest festival takes place: the Feast of the Must.

LAGOON FLORA AND FAUNA

The lagoon abounds in gilt-head bream, sea bass, clams, cuttlefish and crabs, all prey for wetland waterfowl such as swans, egrets, cormorants and the rare black-winged stilts. Sea lavender blooms on land masses, rock samphire clings to crumbling masonry, while glasswort thrives in the salt-ridden marshes.

6 Lazzaretto Nuovo
⊞ H2 ⊞ Apr–Oct
ⓦ lazzarettiveneziani.it ⊡

Up until the 1700s this island, across the water from Sant'Erasmo, served as a quarantine station for merchant ships entering the lagoon and suspected of carrying the plague. Together with Sant'Erasmo it held up to 10,000 people during the 1576 pestilence, while cargoes were fumigated with rosemary and juniper in temporary shelters. Later converted into a military stronghold, it now swarms with archaeology enthusiasts, intent on unearthing the island's secrets, and carefree Italian students attending summer camps. Call ahead to book a guided tour of the island.

7 Burano
⊞ H1

A haven for artists, Burano takes pride in its brightly painted houses, fish and lacemaking (p63). The islanders cherish an old legend about a faithful sailor who resisted the sirens' call and was rewarded with a magnificent veil of magical foam for his bride, which was later worked into lace, a trade that brought worldwide fame and fortune to this isolated fishing community. These days, old women still strain their eyes with patient stitches, but many articles are imported from abroad. Burano's main thoroughfare, Via Baldassare Galuppi, named after the Burano-born composer (1706–85), is still lined with a few traditional lace and linen stalls, alongside outdoor trattorias serving fresh fish. The island's dramatically leaning bell tower is visible from afar.

8 Certosa
⊞ H2

Inhabited by religious communities for over 600 years, the "charterhouse" island lost much of its history during its occupation by French, Austrian and Italian forces, and after it was sold off to wealthy Europeans such as Prince Charles of Prussia. Now, however, the island has been rehabilitated and includes a smart marina, a sailing club and kayak centre, a beautiful park, a hotel and a popular alfresco bar run by the acclaimed chef Raffaelle Alajmo. Alilaguna's Linea Blu boats (alilaguna.it) stop here seasonally. From the Lido–Punta Sabbioni ferry the impressive ramparts of Sanmicheli's 16th-century Forte di Sant'Andrea can be seen, much as they must have appeared in the past to any hostile vessels that dared to enter the lagoon unbidden.

Murano's famed handblown glass sculptures

9 Murano
G2

Long synonymous with glassmaking, Murano brought blowing and fusion techniques to extraordinary heights in the 1500s. So closely guarded were the trade secrets that skilled crafters were forbidden to migrate, on pain of death. Though Venice's glass monopoly lasted just until the 17th century, its fame lives on. A visit to the Museo del Vetro (Glass Museum) with its 4,000 exhibits (p62) is a must. Don't be put off by the reps who invite tourists to see the furnace and showroom; it's a unique opportunity to watch the glassblowers at work and is free. However, if you accept a free boat trip from San Marco to a glass factory, you're expected to make your own way back by vaporetto if you don't buy anything. Glassmaking aside, Murano is a lovely place with canals, alleyways and friendly islanders.

10 Punta Sabbioni
Ferry No. 14 from Lido and S Zaccaria

This locality clings to the promontory extending westwards from the mainland – a continuous string of beach resorts equipped with spacious campsites. Alongside idyllic backwaters and canals is Punta Sabbioni ("big sandy point"), a busy bus-ferry terminal that bustles with summer holidaymakers. It came into being as sand accumulated behind the 1,100-m (3,600-ft) breakwater erected to protect the port mouth and littoral.

Vibrantly coloured houses lining the waterways of Burano

SAILING THE LAGOON

Morning

To save money, buy a one-day travel card and then take a vaporetto from Fondamente Nove to **Murano** to watch a glassmaking demonstration at a furnace or one of the workshops. Don't miss Murano's very own **Grand Canal**, before returning via Fondamenta Manin for the turn-off towards the **Faro** (light-house) landing stage. **Bar al Faro** (Fondamenta Piave 20, Murano) is a perfect spot for coffee.

Take a ferry to **Burano** (p120). Either picnic on the famous Burano biscuits or have lunch at **Da Romano** (Piazza Galuppi 221, Burano; closed Tue & Sun D, mid-Dec–early Feb D), which is a popular meeting place for artists.

Afternoon

Pop over to **Torcello** (p119) by ferry for the awe-inspiring Byzantine mosaics in the basilica. Climb the bell tower for views of the lagoon and the Dolomites, if weather conditions and visibility are favourable.

Take the ferry back to **Burano** (p120) and then head east towards Treporti. A stretch parallel to the littoral separating the lagoon from the Adriatic Sea takes you to **Punta Sabbioni**, where you can stop over for a drink on the jetty.

End the day sailing across the lagoon mouth, via the **Lido** (p124), back to **Piazza San Marco** (p30).

Specialist Shops

1. Cesare Sent
📍 G2 🏠 Fondamenta Vetrai 8B, Murano 🌐 cesaresent.it
This talented artist from a long line of glassmakers transforms the ancient art of murrhine glassware into striking modern objects of beauty.

2. ArtStudio
📍 G2 🏠 Fondamenta Rivalonga 48, Murano 🌐 davidepenso.info
Watch glass artist Davide Penso at work producing marvellous African-inspired glass beads.

3. Manin 56
📍 G2 🏠 Fondamenta Manin 56, Murano 🌐 manin56.com
Striking etched bowls and slender wine glasses from Salviati flank international designer items in this collection.

4. Nason & Moretti
📍 G2 🏠 Calle Dietro Gli Orti 12, Murano 🔒 Sat & Sun 🌐 nasonmoretti.com
This shop stocks a stunning collection of glassware created by acclaimed Murano designers in a dazzling array of colours and styles. It is well worth visiting.

Hand-embroidered lace creations at Lidia Merletti d'Arte

5. Barovier & Toso
📍 G2 🏠 Fondamenta Vetrai 28, Murano 🌐 barovier.com
The oldest family of glassmakers in the world, the Baroviers are able to trace their ancestry back to the 13th century. They still produce stunning contemporary pieces.

6. Mazzega
📍 G2 🏠 Fondamenta da Mula 147, Murano 🌐 mazzega.it
Vast showrooms at Mazzega display traditional and semi-modern glass designs, with an emphasis on chandeliers and vases.

7. CAM
📍 G2 🏠 Piazzale Colonna 1, Murano 🌐 camvetri.com
This is the first shop visitors see as they disembark at the Murano Colonna stop. It is an internationally known firm specializing in distinctive high-quality, modern pieces.

8. Pastificio e Panificio Giorgio Garbo
📍 H1 🏠 Via S Mauro 336, Burano
Sample some *bussolai,* Burano's trademark vanilla-flavoured short-bread, freshly baked in traditional rounds or "S" shapes.

9. Emilia Burano
📍 H1 🏠 Via Galuppi 205, Burano 🌐 emiliaburano.it
Superb laceware and exquisite in-house-designed linen collections are sold at this family-run boutique.

10. Lidia Merletti d'Arte
📍 H1 🏠 Via Galuppi 215, Burano 🌐 dallalidia.it
While the front of this shop is an emporium of lace tablecloths, hand towels and mats, the rear has a gallery with a priceless 18th-century wedding gown, a lace fan owned by Louis XIV and lace altarpieces.

Places to Eat

Enjoying lunch outdoors at the Trattoria da Romano

1. Trattoria Busa alla Torre, Da Lele

🅟 G2 🄰 Campo S Stefano 3, Murano 🄲 041 739 662 🄳 D · €

Dine inside under timber rafters or out in the square. Start with ravioli filled with fish, but leave room for the nougat pastries.

2. Panificio Giovanni Marcato

🅟 G2 🄰 Fondamenta Rivalonga 16, Murano 🄲 041 739 176 🄳 D · €

Pizza with tomato and olives, *zaletti* biscuits and *pincetto* (sponge cake with chocolate) feature on the menu among other delicious offerings.

3. Osteria La Perla Ai Bisatei

🅟 G2 🄰 Campo S Bernardo 6, Murano 🄲 041 739 528 🄳 D & Wed · €

The *fritto misto* seafood is superb at this restaurant offering home-style cooking at reasonable prices. Credit cards are not accepted here.

4. Trattoria Valmarana

🅟 G2 🄰 Fondamenta Navagero 31, Murano 🄲 041 739 313 🄳 D, Sun–Wed & Mon am · €

Rombo al forno con patate e olive (flounder with olives and potatoes) is a speciality at this stylish restaurant with a waterside terrace.

5. Trattoria da Romano

🅟 H1 🄰 Via San Martino Destra 221, Burano 🄲 041 730 030 🄳 Tue, Sun D & mid Oct–mid Apr D · €€€

This family-run trattoria is known for its *risotto di gò*, made with a tiny lagoon fish. It is frequented by celebrities such as Robert De Niro.

6. Riva Rosa Ristorante

🅟 H1 🄰 Via S Mauro 296, Burano 🄲 041 730 850 🄳 Wed, Mon–Fri D · €€€

Try the Rossini aperitivo with freshly juiced strawberries and prosecco at this romantic canalside restaurant.

7. Antica Trattoria alla Maddalena

🅟 H1 🄰 Fondamenta S Caterina 7B, Mazzorbo 🄲 041 730 151 🄳 Thu, Wed D · €

Try the spring artichokes or the roast duck with a light, local white wine at this restaurant. Book in advance.

8. Al Gatto Nero

🅟 H1 🄰 Fondamenta Giudecca 88, Burano 🄲 041 730 120 🄳 Mon; Wed D, Thu & Sun; 1st week in Jul & Nov · €€

This alfresco fish restaurant serves fresh seafood and homemade pasta.

9. Locanda Cipriani

🅟 H1 🄰 Piazza S Fosca 29, Torcello 🄲 041 730 150 🄳 Jan–Feb; Tue & D Sun–Thu & Mar, Nov & Dec · €€€

The house speciality here is *filetto di San Pietro Carlina* (baked John Dory with tomato and capers).

10. Venissa

🅟 H1 🄰 Fondamenta S Caterina 3, Mazzorbo 🄲 041 527 22 81 🄳 Restaurant: Tue & Wed, early Jan–Feb; Osteria: Thu & early Jan–Feb · €€€

Choose between the low-key *osteria* and the sophisticated restaurant serving locally grown produce.

THE SOUTHERN LAGOON AND VENICE LIDO

Sheltered by the Adriatic Sea, the shifting sand spits of the southern lagoon have long transformed into a permanent littoral, the residential Lido, by both natural and human intervention. The latter dates back to as early as the 6th century, but the earth and wicker barriers built then have since been modified into sturdy seawalls and massive breakwaters at the shipping entrances of San Nicolò, Alberoni and Chioggia. On the lagoon's southwestern edge are fish farms and wild shallows where hunters and fishers still roam, well clear of the Valle Averto reserve run by the World Wildlife Fund for Nature (WWF). Closer to Venice is a cluster of islands, including majestic San Giorgio, populous Giudecca and diminutive land masses such as Lazzaretto Vecchio. Once a quarantine zone for plague victims, Lazzaretto Vecchio has been re-adapted as a home for stray dogs. There's also a sanatorium-turned resort here, along with countless other evocative abandoned places.

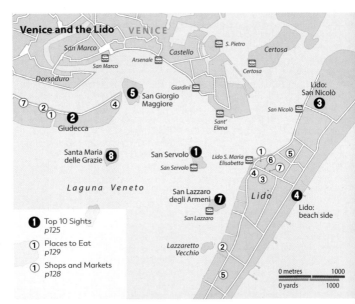

Venice and the Lido

VENICE

San Marco — Dorsoduro — San Marco — Arsenale — Castello — S. Pietro — Certosa — Certosa

Giardini — San Giorgio Maggiore — ⑤

Sant' Elena

Lido: San Nicolò — San Nicolò — ③

⑦ ② ① ② ④
Giudecca

Santa Maria delle Grazie — ⑧

San Servolo ① — San Servolo

Lido S. Maria Elisabetta — ① ⑤ / ⑥ ⑦ / ④ ② ③

Laguna Veneto

San Lazzaro degli Armeni ⑦ — San Lazzaro

Lido

Lido: beach side — ④

Lazzaretto Vecchio — ②

⑤

① **Top 10 Sights** p125

① **Places to Eat** p129

① **Shops and Markets** p128

0 metres — 1000
0 yards — 1000

For places to stay in this area, see p151

Learning painting techniques at San Servolo

1 San Servolo

Ferry No. 20 from San Zaccaria

Halfway between San Marco and the Lido is the island of San Servolo. In 1648, 200 nuns exiled from Candia, Crete, by the Turks were lodged on this island, but after their numbers dwindled in 1725 it was given over to a sanatorium that cared for patients with mild psychiatric ailments. The roomy buildings are now home to the Venice International University and a trade school for artisans from all over Europe.

2 Giudecca
🗺 B6

An S-shaped slice of land facing the sun-blessed Zattere, this residential garden island was first known as "Spinalonga" for its fishbone form. It was renamed either after an early Jewish community or for the *giudicati* (radical aristocrats) exiled here. The famous Italian Renaissance artist Michelangelo spent three peaceful years here in voluntary exile from 1529. Much later it became an important industrial zone with shipbuilding and the immense Molino Stucky flour mill. Usually quiet and neighbourly, it comes to life with a vengeance for the mid-July Redentore festivities *(p80)*.

3 Lido: San Nicolò

The northern end of the Lido littoral, a key point in the Republic's defence, used to be equipped with impressive naval fortifications, including chains that would be laid across the lagoon mouth as a deterrent to invaders. The historic Festa della Sensa celebration *(p80)* is held offshore from the church of San Nicolò, founded in 1044 and a former Benedictine monastery, now a study centre. Also worth visiting is the 1386 Jewish cemetery that recounts the cultures of the Venetian Jewish community. Visits are only by guided tour between May and October; call 041 715 359 to book. Alternatively, take a 35-minute cruise on the car ferry between Tronchetto and San Nicolò.

4 Lido: Beach Side
🗺 H2

Manicured sand, raked daily, and neat rows of multicoloured bathing cabins and beach umbrellas sum up the Lido from June to September, made famous in Thomas Mann's novel *Death in Venice (p59)*. Venetians spend their summers socializing in style here. Things liven up considerably for the ten-day International Film Festival in September, when the shady streets are filled with film buffs and critics on bicycles.

The Southern Lagoon

Venice

Area shown to left

Fusina

Laguna Veneto

③

⑥ Malamocco

Alberoni

Golfo di Venezia

⑥ ⑨ San Pietro in Volta

⑨ Pellestrina

⑧ ⑨ ⑩
⑧ ⑨ ⑩
⑩ Chioggia

0 km   3
0 miles   3

A gondola on St Mark's Basin with San Giorgio Maggiore in the background

5 San Giorgio Maggiore

📍 F5 🏛 Isola di S Giorgio Maggiore 🕐 Apr–Oct: 9am–7pm daily; Nov–Mar: 8:30am–6pm daily 🌐 visitcini.com 🚻♿

This island is separated from the main body of Venice by St Mark's Basin and retains a meditative air. It is home to a 16th-century landmark church (p54) by Andrea Palladio (p61), adjoining an elegant Benedictine monastery. Today, the monastery is a thriving Venetian cultural foundation, hosting concerts, international events and exhibitions. At the rear is the open-air Teatro Verde, which is used for performances of contemporary dance and music.

6 Lido: Malamocco

📍 H2

About midway along the Lido is the pretty, quiet village of Malamocco. It's now hard to imagine that it was the most important lagoon settlement soon after Roman times and the main port for Padua. A storm and giant waves washed away the entire town in 1106, but it was later rebuilt in the vicinity on a smaller scale. It is appreciated for its 15th-century buildings, peaceful nature and rustic trattorias.

7 San Lazzaro degli Armeni

📍 G2 🕐 By appointment only 🌐 mechitar.org 🚻♿

Venice made a gift of this erstwhile leper colony to the Armenian monk, the Venerable Mechitar, who had fled his native country to escape Ottoman persecution. Intent on fostering the Armenian culture and language, he founded a religious community in San Lazzaro called the Armenian Mechitarist Congregation, and set up a printing press that ran until 1994. Multilingual monks instruct visitors in Armenian history and lead tours through a small museum housing archaeological and artistic finds from the community. The library, which contains over 100,000 volumes and precious illuminated manuscripts, can also be visited.

8 Santa Maria delle Grazie

📍 G2

Close to San Giorgio Maggiore, this abandoned island used to be a hospice for pilgrims. It was named after a miraculous image of the Virgin brought back from Constantinople and attributed to St Luke. Its colourful history features a series of religious orders and churches, devastating fires, allotments

---

HEYDAY OF THE LIDO

The Lido was Europe's leading seaside resort at the turn of the 20th century. Evidence of its glory and popularity can still be seen in the magnificent Art Deco villas. Exemplary survivors are the Hotel des Bains and the Excelsior, built in 1907 as the world's largest hotel, complete with mock minarets. Before this, the Lido was appreciated for its healthy air.

and luxuriant gardens. It ultimately became the site of the city's infectious diseases hospital. It is now private property with no public access.

9 San Pietro in Volta and Pellestrina

🗺 F1

This narrow 11-km (6.5-mile) central strip of land, linked to the Lido and Chioggia by ferry, is dotted with picturesque fishing communities, once famous for lacemaking and now renowned for champion rowers and a shipyard. The Genoese wiped out the villages during the 14th century, an event almost repeated during the disastrous 1966 floods – powerful waves broke over the seawall, forcing full-scale evacuation. The massive defensive barriers with their 14-m (46-ft) broad base were first erected in the 1700s, but have consequently needed large-scale reinforcement.

10 Chioggia

🗺 F1

A lively fishing town, Chioggia has elegant bridges over navigable canals. The friendly inhabitants have a reputation for lawlessness and bickering, and speak a distinctive dialect with a singsong inflection. Chioggia's greatest moment came as the arena for the decisive battle in the 1378–9 war, when the Genoese came close to conquering Venice. In flat-bottomed boats the crafty locals lured the enemy into the lagoon, thus gaining the upper hand. Its bustling fish market (every morning except Monday) is a good reason to come here.

Cleaning fishing nets, a daily ritual in Chioggia

A DAY ON THE LAGOON

(map showing:)
Malamocco
Alberoni
BUS
FERRY
Laguna Veneto
San Pietro in Volta
Golfo di Venezia
BUS
FERRY
Pellestrina
FERRY
Chioggia

Morning

From the Santa Maria Elisabetta ferry stop, either hire a bicycle or take bus B southwest along the lagoon edge for **Malamocco**. Wander through the peaceful village and over its bridge to the sea to take in the Adriatic and the impressive seawall. Then proceed with buses B or 11 through Alberoni and past the golf course for the vehicle ferry across the lagoon entrance. Get off at the second stop for **San Pietro in Volta**. Climb the high seawall for panoramic views of the sea, before turning lagoon-wards for views of the pastel-painted fishing settlement that spreads along the waterfront.

Have lunch at one of the many trattorias (p129) or a sandwich and glass of wine at one of the modest waterfront bars.

Afternoon

Further south the bus terminates at **Pellestrina**, a brightly painted fishing village flanked by an active shipyard. The passenger ferry to **Chioggia** is a beautiful half-hour cruise via the Ca' Roman landing stage, which provides access to a beach. Chioggia is a lovely town to explore, with its traffic-free piazza lined with old palazzos and countless fish restaurants.

Indulge in a pre-dinner drink and some *cicchetti* at one of the cafés in the elegant Corso del Popolo.

Shops and Markets

Motorbikes parked outside OVS & Conad

1. Gardin Bike

📍 H2 🏠 Piazzale Santa Maria Elisabetta 2/A Lido 🔽 biciclette gardin.com

This well-stocked bike shop rents out all normal steeds as well as four-wheeler family models.

2. General Market

📍 H2 🏠 Via Falier, Lido 🕐 Tue am

Fresh produce is sold from vans, alongside designer-quality clothes, shoes and bags at reasonable prices. The lagoon setting makes a trip to this market worthwhile.

3. La Spiga Erboristeria

📍 H2 🏠 Via Lepanto 5, Lido 🕐 Sun & Mon

You will find Erbolario natural beauty products and plant-based cosmetics, as well as natural remedies for minor ailments here.

4. Salumeria Da Ciano

📍 H2 🏠 Via del Gallo, 156/A, Lido 🕐 Sun pm 🔽 salumeriadaciano.it

This delicatessen stocks gourmet Italian food products including mozzarella, ham, handmade pasta and artisan biscuits. Fresh ready-made Italian dishes can also be bought.

5. Arbor

📍 H2 🏠 Gran Viale Santa Maria Elisabetta 10, Lido 🔽 arbor collective.com

The range of snow-, skate-, and formal-wear at this shop attracts both foreign and Italian customers.

6. OVS & Conad

📍 H2 🏠 Gran Viale Santa Maria Elisabetta 21/B, Lido 🔽 ovsfashion.com

OVS, a store with fashionable, moderately priced clothing for all ages, is combined with Conad, a supermarket with a great selection of fresh produce.

7. Benetton

📍 H2 🏠 Gran Viale Santa Maria Elisabetta 47/A, Lido 🕐 Sun 🔽 it.benetton.com

This small shop is well-stocked with underwear, nightwear and swimwear.

8. El Penelo

📍 F2 🏠 577 Borgo San Giovanni, Chioggia 🕐 Wed & Sun

Owner Giorgio Boscolo is an expert in crafting traditional fishers' clay pipes – and is the only artisan who still makes them in terracotta and coloured glazes.

9. Venturini Souvenirs

📍 F1 🏠 Corso del Popolo 1349, Chioggia 🔽 venturinisouvenirs.it

Ignore the trinkets here and instead focus on the hand-crafted models of colourful *bragozzo* boats (p36).

10. Panificio Da Sergio

📍 F1 🏠 Stradale Ponte Caneva 626, Chioggia 🕐 Mon

The dry biscuits sold at this store were traditionally made for seafarers. *Pevarini*, spicy rings with molasses and aniseed, and *Dolce del Doge*, a type of cake, are their delectable specialities.

Places to Eat

1. Trattoria Altanella
📍 E6 🏠 Calle delle Erbe, Giudecca 268 ☎ 041 522 77 80 🕙 Mon & Tue, Jan & Dec · €€€

Treat yourself to a candlelit dinner on the terrace. Fish dishes such as *frittura mista* (assorted fried seafood) are worth trying.

2. Ai Cacciatori
📍 D6 🏠 Fondamenta Ponte Piccolo Giudecca 320 ☎ 041 528 58 49 🕙 Mon, 15 Dec–15 Jan · €€€

Enjoy hearty Venetian fare such as *gnocchi con nero di seppia* (potato dumplings with cuttlefish ink) in canalside seating with lovely views.

3. Trattoria da Scarso
📍 H2 🏠 Piazzale Malamocco 5, Malamocco 🕙 Hours vary, check website 🌐 trattoriadascarso.it · €

The family-run Trattoria Scarso has a lovely garden hung with fishing nets.

4. Trattoria La Battigia
📍 H2 🏠 Via Nicosia 10, Lido 🕙 Mon 🌐 trattorialabattigia.com · €€

Renowned for its traditional fish dishes and friendly atmosphere, this trattoria is the place to enjoy *schie con* polenta, gray shrimps typical of the Venetian lagoon.

5. Hotel Cipriani
📍 E6 🏠 Guidecca 10 🕙 Nov–Mar 🌐 belmond.com · €€€

Savour an artistic tasting menu at Michelin-starred Oro Restaurant,

PRICE CATEGORIES

For a three-course meal for one with half a bottle of wine (or equivalent meal), taxes and extra charges.

€ under €40 €€ €40–60 €€€ over €60

sip a mocktail at Cip's Club, or dine at rustic Giudecca 10 – Hotel Cipriani *(p151)* is the perfect venue for every mood.

6. Ristorante da Memo
📍 Via Portosecco 157, S Pietro in Volta ☎ 041 527 91 25 🕙 Tue, Nov–Mar · €€

Try the fresh shrimps, eel or sole at this modest outdoor restaurant.

7. Harry's Dolci
📍 C6 🏠 Fondamenta S Biagio, Giudecca 773 🕙 Nov–Easter 🌐 cipriani.com · €€€

With views across the Giudecca Canal, this is the "sweet" branch of Harry's Bar *(p35)* serving sorbets and pastries.

8. Ristorante La Sgura
📍 F1 🏠 Fondamenta Marangoni 1295, Chioggia ☎ 041 403 232 🕙 Sun D, Mon, Jan · €€

Situated on a quiet canal, this place also has a great selection of meat. Try the *zuppa di pesce* (fish soup).

9. Ristorante El Gato
📍 F1 🏠 Corso del Popolo 653, Chioggia 🕙 Mon & Tue, 15–28 Feb 🌐 gattonero.com · €€

This restaurant serves superb *frittura* (fried fish), fish risotto and sautéed mussels and clams.

10. Trattoria La Nassa
📍 F1 🏠 Calle Ponte Caneva 625, Chioggia 🕙 Wed 🌐 gattonero.com · €

This family-run restaurant serves a good selection of raw seafood dishes.

Diners enjoying the sunset from the terrace, Harry's Dolci

PADUA, VICENZA AND VERONA

A wealth of art cities punctuate the fertile Veneto plain, which stretches in a broad wedge north from the Po River to the foothills of the Dolomites. The presence of the Romans and Venetians in the region is evident in the fascinating amphitheatres and elegant palaces in Verona and Vicenza, both of which have been declared UNESCO World Heritage Sites. Amid vineyards of grapes, pressed for light sparkling prosecco and aromatic Bardolino, are charming villas with ornamental gardens. Each town has its distinctive character: Padua, a business hub but with an artistic and religious heart; Vicenza, famous for its goldsmiths and Andrea Palladio's architecture; and romantic Verona, lazing on the banks of the mighty Adige River as it flows south swollen with snow-melt from the Alps. Each city can easily be visited as day-trips from Venice by train.

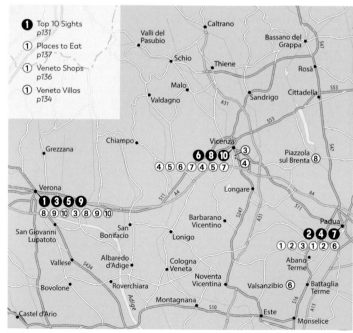

1 Top 10 Sights
p131

1 Places to Eat
p137

1 Veneto Shops
p136

1 Veneto Villas
p134

For places to stay in this area, see p151

1 Verona Arena

🏛 Piazza Brà, Verona ⏰ 9am–7pm Tue–Sun 🌐 arena.it 📷

This massive Roman amphitheatre dating from the 1st century CE measures almost 140 m (460 ft) in length. The impressive arcades and 44-level tiered seating for 22,000 people, that once rang with the cries of gladiator fights, now echo with arias from operas during the popular summer festival. Verdi's *Aïda* has opened the festival every year since 1913. Visitors should note that the opening hours are shorter during the opera festival in the summer.

2 Cappella degli Scrovegni

🏛 Piazza Eremitani, Padua ⏰ 9am–7pm daily 🌐 cappella degliscrovegni.it

The sky-blue vault studded with gold stars in this glorious Paduan chapel

Giotto's *Last Judgement* at the Cappella degli Scrovegni

seems to hover over Giotto's vibrant frescoes, which narrate the lives of Mary and Jesus. The Florentine artist (1266–1337) was summoned by Enrico Scrovegni to work on the chapel in 1305–6, to atone for the sins of his late father, a moneylender. Noteworthy among the 38 distinct scenes is the *Last Judgement* on the entrance wall, with its ranks of haloed and shield-bearing angels. Booking is essential all year round and required well in advance in summer. Visits last 30 to 35 minutes and include a 15-minute wait in the "decontamination" chamber.

3 Casa di Giulietta

🏛 Via Cappello 23, Verona ⏰ 9am–7pm Tue–Sun 🌐 casadi giulietta.comune.verona.it 📷

Visitors flock to "Juliet's House", the 13th-century presumed abode of the Shakespearean heroine, complete with a pretty balcony (added in 1928) from which you may imagine her uttering that immortal cry: "O Romeo, Romeo, wherefore art thou Romeo?" The courtyard walls are filled with graffiti left by lovers from all over the world.

4 Basilica del Santo

🏛 Piazza del Santo, Padua ⏰ 9am–1pm & 2–6pm Tue–Sun 🌐 basilicadelsanto.org

Popularly known as "il Santo", Padua's revered pilgrimage site was built in the 13th century to house the remains of St Anthony, a Franciscan monk from Portugal. His tomb is encircled by burning candles and his tongue is guarded separately in a reliquary in the Treasury, recovered after being stolen. The Treasury also has artworks by Sansovino, Tiepolo and Titian (*p60*).

5 Museo di Storia Naturale
🏛 Lungadige Porta Vittoria 9, Verona 🕐 10am–6pm Tue–Sun (last adm: 5:30pm) 🌐

Gigantic ferns, weird fish and an ancestor of the crocodile, all in fossilized form from the Eocene era 50 million years ago, are among the treasures displayed here. Hailing from Bolca in the Lessini foothills, they testify to the tropical shallows that spread across the area prior to the formation of the Alps.

6 Palazzo Leoni Montanari
🏛 Contra' Santa Corona 25, Vicenza 🕐 10am–6pm Tue–Sun 🌐 gallerieditalia.com 🌐

On the entrance portal of this lavish Baroque palace are carvings of writhing serpents; Hercules is shown in the act of slaying the Hydra on the loggia. The gallery's masterpieces include 120 Russian icons and 14 fascinating paintings by Pietro Longhi depicting scenes from 18th-century Venetian life.

7 Palazzo Bo
🏛 Via VIII Febbraio 2, Padua 🕐 Daily: for tours only 🌐 unipd.it/visitebo 🌐🌐

The original lectern where Galileo Galilei held his lessons between 1592 and 1610 can be seen on the guided tour of Padua's historic university, founded in 1222 and second only to Bologna as Italy's and the world's oldest. The institution houses the world's first anatomy theatre (1594) where dissections had to be carried out in secret as the church forbade such practices. Other illustrious scholars of the university have included astronomer Copernicus (1473–1543), Gabriel Fallopius (1523–62), who discovered the function of the Fallopian tubes and Elena Lucrezia Corner Piscopia (p56) – the world's first woman graduate.

8 Piazza dei Signori
🏛 Basilica Palladiana: Piazza dei Signori, Vicenza 🕐 During exhibitions 🌐

In addition to the cafés in Vicenza's main square, visitors can admire the buildings by Palladio, whose

---

ROMEO AND JULIET

There is no doubt that the Capulet and Montague families existed, though they were probably more friendly than William Shakespeare made out in his 1594–5 tragedy. The world's most famous star-crossed lovers may have come from Vicenza, the home town of Luigi Da Porto, who was the author of the original 1530 account.

Piazza dei Signori in Vicenza, with its basilica

16th-century designs went on to influence both his home town and architecture worldwide (p61). The basilica, in particular, is impressive with twin levels of colonnaded arches. A statue of the architect can be found in the piazzetta at the western end.

9 Piazza delle Erbe
🏛 Torre dei Lamberti, Cortile Mercato Vecchio, Verona ⏱ 10am–6pm Mon–Fri, 11am–7pm Sat & Sun (last adm: 45 min before closing) 🌐 torredeilamberti.it

Originally Verona's Roman forum, this square is still a great spot for discussing business over a coffee. Parasols shade souvenirs at the market, watched over by a winged lion atop a column, a vestige of Venetian domination. The 84-m (275-ft) Torre dei Lamberti offers great city views.

10 Teatro Olimpico
🏛 Piazza Matteotti 11, Vicenza ⏱ Sep–Jun: 9am–5pm Tue–Sun; Jul & Aug: 10am–6pm (last adm: 30 min before closing) 🌐 teatrolimpico vicenza.it 🔗

A castle courtyard draped with creepers was chosen for this Vicenza theatre, designed by Palladio. The performing area is based on a Roman model, while the stage scenery represents the city of Thebes, built for 1585's inaugural play, Sophocles' Oedipus Rex. Scaled statues and varying stage levels create clever tricks of perspective.

The elliptical-shaped anatomical theatre at Palazzo Bo

A DAY OUT IN VERONA

Morning
Where better to begin than the inspiring **Verona Arena**, where, as entertainment, wild animals once made a meal of gladiators? Afterwards, relax in the sun with a creamy coffee at **Liston 12 Caffè** (Piazza Brà 12, Verona; 045 803 11 68) and dig into a freshly baked jam-filled croissant.

A short stroll leads past the boutiques in Via Mazzini. Paved with pink-tinged limestone embedded with ammonite fossils, this street leads to **Casa di Giulietta** to the right, or **Piazza delle Erbe's** palaces to the left.

Backtrack to Via Mazzini for lunch at **Ristorante Greppia** (Vicolo Samaritana 3, Verona; 045 800 45 77; closed Mon) for bollito misto (mixed boiled meat) served with a traditional peppery sauce.

Afternoon
Head over the Adige River via the ancient Ponte di Pietra to the **Teatro Romano** on Via Rigaste Redentore – well worth a visit even if you're not in town for a performance. Then follow the river or walk back through town towards the medieval **Ponte Scaligero**. The triple-arched construction was blown up by the German army in World War II, then rebuilt brick by brick by residents.

The bridge leads to **Castelvecchio** where you can grab an aperitivo at any of the welcoming bars.

Veneto Villas

1. Villa Barbaro

⌂ Via Cornuda 7, Maser ⌚ Apr–Oct: 10am–6pm Tue–Sun; Nov–Mar: 11am–5pm Sat, Sun & public hols 🅦 villadimaser.it 🎟

The best preserved villa (1560) by Palladio (p61) lies close to the pretty hill town of Asolo. This charming country house features all manner of Roman-inspired elements, from the nymphaeum and grotto to the circular temple akin to the Pantheon. Playful *trompe l'oeil* frescoes by Veronese (p60) adorn the six main rooms, counting among the most important works of art of the Venetian Renaissance. The garden is punctuated with Classical statuary. Drop in to the estate's wine cellar in a farm house next door for wine tastings.

2. Villa Pisani – La Nazionale

⌂ Via Doge Pisani 7, Strà ⌚ Hours vary, check website 🅦 villapisani.beniculturali.it 🎟

This splendid two-floor 18th-century villa designed for Doge Alvise Pisani has 114 sumptuously furnished rooms and a ballroom decorated by Tiepolo. Above the huge façade columns, scores of statues line the roof overlooking inner courtyards and a spacious park where the Venetian nobility would promenade. Be sure to explore the wonderful 1721 circular maze. The guest list has included one-time proprietor Napoleon, Russian and Austrian royalty, and Mussolini.

Baroque façade of the Villa Pisani – La Nazionale

3. Villa Valmarana "Ai Nani"

⌂ Via dei Nani 8, Vicenza ⌚ Mar–Oct: 10am–6pm daily (Nov–Feb: to 4pm Mon–Fri, to 5pm Sat & Sun) 🅦 villavalmarana.com 🎟

Known for the statues of dwarfs on the garden wall, these cosy twin buildings, built by the Valmarana family, stand on a pretty ridge looking up to Monte Berico and its sanctuary. The Tiepolo father-and-son fresco team were invited here by Count Valmarana in 1757 to decorate the main part and the guest quarters.

4. Villa Valmarana "La Rotonda"

⌂ Via Rotonda 45, Vicenza ⌚ Hours vary, check website 🅦 villalarotonda.it 🎟🎟

The perfectly proportioned imposing Villa Valmarana with four temple façades sits on a hill overlooking the architect Palladio's adoptive town of Vicenza. The house has been imitated throughout the world. If you want to visit the villa itself as opposed to the rather limited grounds, beware it's only open three days a week.

5. Villa Foscari "La Malcontenta"

⌂ Via dei Turisti 9, Malcontenta ⌚ Apr–Oct: 9am–noon & 2:30–5:30pm Fri–Wed 🅦 lamalcontenta.com 🎟

Located on the bend of the Brenta Canal, but now rather too close to the Marghera industrial area, this wonderful residence designed by Andrea Palladio in 1571 is one of his best-known creations. It has a Greek temple façade, while the interior is decorated with frescoes. The name is said to refer to the "discontent" of a female member of the Foscari family, exiled here for adultery. To visit, it's essential that you book in advance.

A tastefully decorated room at the Villa Emo in Fanzolo

6. Villa Barbarigo
🏠 Galzignano, Valsanzibio
🕐 Mar–Nov: 10am–sunset daily
🌐 valsanzibiogiardino.it ⚡

The Euganean Hills are the setting for this Baroque garden, designed for the Venetian Barbarigo family by Luigi Bernini, architect of the Vatican fountains in Rome. The villa, dating from 1669, is a private dwelling, but the 15-ha (37-acre) garden provides a boxwood maze, fountains, fish ponds and statues. There's also a kiosk offering a good selection of snacks and drinks.

7. Villa Emo
🏠 Via Stazione 5, Fanzolo di Vedelago
🕐 Mar–Oct: 10am–6pm Wed–Sun (last adm: 5pm); Nov–Feb: 10am–4pm Thu–Sun (last adm: 3pm)
🌐 villaemo.org

Another of Palladio's light-flooded country residences, this villa was built for the Emo family in around 1560. A harmonious central block is flanked by graceful arched *barchesse* (wings), designed for storing hay and farm tools. The interior has lively frescoes by Renaissance artist Zelotti, who is also responsible for the decorations in Villa Malcontenta. The frescoes show the love lives of ancient Greek deities.

8. Villa Contarini
🏠 Piazzola sul Brenta
🕐 Mar–Oct: 9am–7pm Thu–Tue; Nov–Feb: 10am–4pm Thu–Tue
🌐 villacontarini.eu ⚡

A horseshoe plaza lined with terraced houses faces the façade of this 17th-century country villa, which was once the focus for a thriving farming community. A remarkable system of acoustics was invented so that musicians performing in the Sala della Musica on the first floor could be clearly heard downstairs. An antiques market is held in the grounds on the last Sunday of each month.

9. Villa Cornaro
🏠 Via Roma 35, Piombino Dese
🕐 May–Sep: 3:30–6pm Sat ⚡

This unusual, double-tiered creation by Palladio dates from between 1560 and 1570. The façade columns are both Doric and Corinthian in style, with acanthus leaves or scrolls around the capitals. The interior features over a hundred frescoes by Mattio Bortoloni, which depict various scenes from the Bible. There are also portraits of figures who were significant to the original family, including Catherine Cornaro (Queen of Cyprus) and Admiral Cornaro.

10. Barchessa Valmarana
🏠 Via Valmarana 11, Mira
🕐 Hours vary, check website
🌐 villavalmarana.net ⚡

Formerly guest quarters, these are extant "wings" of a 17th-century villa, whose main body – built in the 16th century by the Dolfin family – was demolished in 1908. Close by are locks on the Brenta waterway, which have been excavated over centuries to divert the river away from the lagoon and eliminate the problem of silting. The building also features wonderful frescoes, which were restored in 1964.

Veneto Shops

A range of items on display at the Coin department store

1. Pasticceria Gelateria Al Duomo

🏠 Via Vandelli 2, Padua 🕐 Tue

This pastry shop has been serving the finest *frittelle* (apple fritters) in town for decades. It is located on the southern corner of the square by the Duomo.

2. Drogheria ai Due Catini d'Oro Dal Zio

🏠 Piazza dei Frutti 46, Padua
🕐 Sun & Mon

Strong mints, peppery Veneto *mostarda* chutney and even feather dusters, among many other things, are sold at this old-fashioned shop.

3. Lo Scarabocchio Di Cestari Arrigo

🏠 Via Ponte Pietra 25, Verona
🕐 Sun & Mon

Find artisanal clothing and accessories at this contemporary boutique.

4. Antica Pasticceria di Sorarù

🏠 Piazzetta Palladio 17, Vicenza
🕐 Wed

This pastry shop is lined with almond and chocolate delicacies, as well as special goodies such as the dove-shaped *colomba* cake at Easter.

5. Cappelleria Palladio

🏠 Piazzetta Palladio 13, Vicenza
🕐 Sun, Mar–Oct: Mon am
🌐 cappelleriapalladio.com

Run by a friendly couple with a 40-year passion for millinery, this charming old-fashioned shop is a hat-lover's heaven. It is in great demand for stylish weddings in the country villas *(p134)*.

6. LaFeltrinelli

🏠 Via S Francesco 7, Padua

Visitors will enjoy browsing the stocked shelves of mystery novels, classics, children's literature and reference books in this chain bookshop.

7. Il Ceppo

🏠 Corso Palladio 196, Vicenza
🕐 Mon 🌐 ilceppovicenza.it

A gourmet's paradise, Il Ceppo has takeaway dishes, pickles and preserves. Buy a catered picnic with wine or a crusty roll filled with Asiago cheese or *sopressa* (salami) sausage.

8. De Rossi "Il Fornaio"

🏠 Corso Porta Borsari 3, Verona
🕐 Mon

A range of pastries and breads is available here. Try the *zaletto* (a biscuit baked with pine nuts and sultanas), and *Baci di Giulietta* (Juliet's Kisses) – almond paste shaped into pursed lips.

9. Mercante d'Oriente

🏠 Corso Sant'Anastasia 34, Verona
🕐 Sun & Mon

Akin to a museum, this antiques dealer dazzles with Chinese and Japanese marvels, Pre-Columbian pieces and traditional and contemporary carpets.

10. Coin

🏠 Via Cappello 30, Verona

This wonderful department store with a good range of casual clothes, cosmetics and home furnishings is right in the centre of town.

Places to Eat

1. Graziati
Piazza della Frutta 40, Padua
049 875 10 14 · Wed · €

Light and buttery *millefoglie* (puff) pastries perfectly accompany the strong, sweet coffee as you sit outside on the lively market square. Light lunches are served downstairs.

2. Caffè Pedrocchi
Via VIII Febbraio 15, Padua
caffepedrocchi.it · €

This 1831 Neo-Classical coffee house was long known as the "café without doors" because it never closed. Liberals of the 19th century would often meet and debate here.

3. Osteria dal Capo
Via Degli Obizzi 2, Padua · Sun & Mon L · osteriadalcapo.it · €

There are plenty of traditional Venetian dishes to try here, such as *zuppa nella pagnotta* (soup in the loaf) and blue cheese *gnocchi*.

4. Antico Guelfo
Contrà Pedemuro San Biagio 90, Vicenza · Tue & Sun evening · ristoranteanticogafaro.it · €€

This central, upmarket restaurant offers superb gluten-free cuisine and an excellent selection of wines.

5. Osteria Il Cursore
Strada Pozzetto 10, Vicenza
044 432 35 04 · Tue · €

Tuck into traditional, seasonal cuisine at this atmospheric restaurant, accompanied by the best local and national wines.

6. Bar Borsa
Piazza dei Signori 26, Vicenza
044 454 45 83 · €

With live music and DJs, hip Borsa attracts a lively crowd. Outdoor seating is on Piazza dei Signori as well as Piazza delle Erbe. It has an all-day menu and offers brunch at weekends.

PRICE CATEGORIES

For a three-course meal for one with half a bottle of wine (or equivalent meal), taxes and extra charges.

€ under €40 €€ €40–60 €€€ over €60

---

7. Angolo Palladio
Piazzetta Palladio 12, Vicenza
044 432 77 90 · Mon–Fri L · €€

This pizzeria-cum-restaurant serves excellent *baccalà* (salt cod) and features an extensive wine list.

8. Ristorante Greppia
Vicolo Samaritana 3, Verona · Mon, 15–31 Jan · ristorantegreppia.it · €

The unforgettable Greppia specializes in *bollito misto*, a selection of nine melt-in-the-mouth meats served with peppery *Perà* sauce.

9. Arche
Via Arche Scaligere 6, Verona
Mon, Sun D, 2 weeks in Jan · ristorantearche.it · €–€€€

Beloved since 1879, Arche's menu features a variety of fish dishes.

10. Antica Bottega del Vino
Vicolo Scudo di Francia 3, Verona
bottegavini.it · €€

Dating to 1890, this restaurant holds 2,500 wines in its cellar. The favourite dish among aficionados is *pastissada de caval*, a dark, spicy horse-meat stew.

Neo-Classical Caffè Pedrocchi, the oldest café in Padua

STREETSMART

Gondolas in Venice

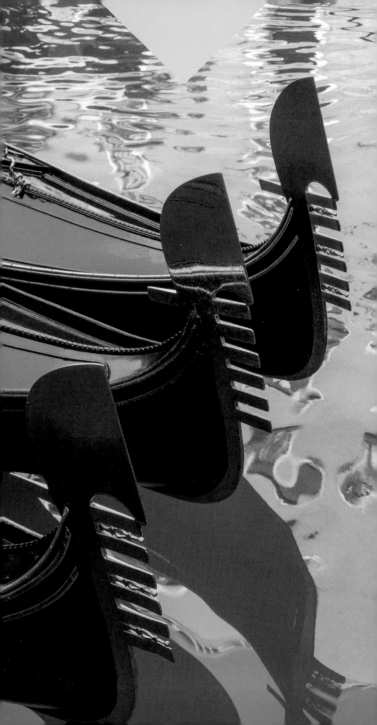

GETTING AROUND

With its canals and waterways, and no cars or buses within the city limits, Venice is unlike many destinations when it comes to exploring. Here is everything you need to know to navigate the city.

TRAVEL COSTS

VAPORETTO

€9.50

One way; valid for 75 minutes

TRAGHETTO

€2

Single trip

GONDOLA

€80

Max six people for 30 minutes

SPEED LIMITS IN VENETO

MOTORWAY	DUAL CARRIAGEWAYS
130 km/h (80 mph)	**100** km/h (60 mph)

NATIONAL ROADS	URBAN AREAS
80 km/h (50 mph)	**50** km/h (30 mph)

Arriving by Air

The main international airport, Aeroporto di Venezia Marco Polo (Venice Marco Polo Airport) is situated 14 km (9 miles) from Venice on the shores of the Venetian Lagoon, just a short bus or boat ride away from the city. A secondary, much smaller airport, Aeroporto di Treviso Antonio Canova (Treviso Antonio Canova Airport), is located 40 km (25 miles) north of Venice. This airport is popular for charter flights and some European budget airlines, including Ryanair, which offers a convenient connecting coach service with Piazzale Roma, Venice's major bus terminal.

To transfer to the city from Marco Polo Airport, you can travel by bus, airport shuttle or taxi, or go by boat from the airport boathouse, in a vaporetto or water taxi. There is little point in hiring a car from the airport, as Venice is a totally car-free city.

For those visiting the Veneto, Valerio Catullo Airport, in Verona, receives direct flights from the UK, other European countries and Africa. A bus service connects to Verona city centre, and costs around €6 each way.

International Train Travel

Italy's train network is operated by **Trenitalia** and **Italo**. Regular high-speed trains connect the main towns and cities of the Veneto to the rest of Italy, Austria, Germany, France and Eastern Europe. Reservations for these services are essential.
Italo
w italotreno.it
Trenitalia
w trenitalia.com

Train Travel in Venice and the Veneto

The easiest and most convenient way to get around the Veneto is by rail. Trenitalia runs an extensive and efficient network throughout the region, and the cost of travel is very reasonable. Services range from the slow *regionale*, which stops at every station en route, through the various intercity trains to the high-speed Freccia and Eurostar, which link Venice with Verona Porta Nuova and beyond.

Direct lines serve **Venezia Santa Lucia** (Venice's main railway station) and **Venezia Mestre** from numerous northern Italian towns including Bologna, Florence, Milan and Verona. Both stations are extremely busy, with over 450 trains arriving in Venice daily.

Train tickets must be validated before boarding by stamping them in machines at the entrance to platforms. Heavy fines are levied if you are caught on board with an unvalidated ticket.

Venezia Mestre
W veneziamestre.it
Venezia Santa Lucia
W veneziasantalucia.it

Long-Distance Bus Travel

An inexpensive way to travel to Venice is by coach. **BUS Italia** offers reasonably priced coach travel throughout Italy. You can buy tickets on board, and services usually depart from outside main railway stations or from the main piazza of smaller towns or cities. **FlixBus** is a low-cost intercity coach network with direct services to Venice from Florence, Milan, Naples, Rome and Turin, as well as from international destinations. Coaches into Venice arrive at the main bus terminus in Piazzale Roma.

BUS Italia
W fsbusitalia.it
FlixBus
W flixbus.com

Cruise Travel

If you do choose to arrive in Venice by cruise ship, it's important to be aware of the issues that surround this popular mode of transport.

Venetians have a complicated relationship with cruising vessels. Although they do provide local jobs, the average cruise liner emits as much pollution as 14,000 cars, damages the already fragile lagoon environment and brings in an unmanageable number of visitors to this tiny city. While the city's plight is often overlooked by the Italian government, the *No Grandi Navi* (no big ships) campaign – which calls to ban large cruise ships entering the lagoon – received support from UNESCO, who threatened to put Venice and its lagoon on its list of endangered heritage sites unless the ban went ahead. On 1 August 2021, an Italian government decree banned massive cruise ships (weighing over 25,000 tonnes) from entering the Giudecca Canal. It is still undecided where these larger ships will be allowed to dock in future. As a short-term solution, in 2022, a temporary berthing facility was inaugurated at Marghera (an industrial zone on the mainland). Smaller cruise ships dock at San Basilio (in Giudecca canal) and Santa Marta (near the mouth of the Giudecca canal), but are also allowed to dock at Marittima (near the Santa Lucia railway station).

Santa Marta and San Basilio are served by vaporetto line 6, which terminates at the Lido. The Marittima is served by the automated People Mover, which takes passengers to the Piazzale Roma in the historic centre and the Tronchetto parking island.

GETTING TO AND FROM VENICE MARCO POLO AIRPORT		
Public transport	**Journey time**	**Fare**
Airport Bus Express (ATVO)	35 mins	€8
Public Bus (ACTV)	21 mins	€8
Water bus (Alilaguna)	30 mins	€15
Taxi	20 mins	€40
Water Taxi	20 mins	€105–135

Public Transport

No cars, buses or bicycles are allowed in Venice's streets; boats are the city's main mode of transport. Venice's transit authority, the **ACTV**, operates three different types of waterbus (*vaporetti, motoscafi* and *motonavi*) plus a network of buses on the Lido and the mainland.

Each city in the Veneto has its own public transport provider. Verona is served by **ATV**, Padua by **APS Holding**, Vicenza by **SVT** and Belluno and the surrounding area by **Dolimiti Bus**. Their websites provide timetables, ticket information, maps, and more.

ACTV
🅦 actv.it
APS Holding
🅦 apsholding.it
ATV
🅦 atv.verona.it
Dolimiti Bus
🅦 dolomitibus.it
SVT
🅦 svt.vi.it

VAPORETTO ROUTES

LINE 1
Zigzag leisurely down the Grand Canal, calling at 20 stops between Piazzale Roma and the Lido.

LINE 2
Take a circular route from San Zaccaria (one stop on from Piazza San Marco) via the Giudecca Canal and Tronchetto, then back down the Grand Canal to Rialto or San Marco.

LINE 4.1
Travel around Venice anti-clockwise on the outer side of the city, then to Murano and back via the Cannaregio Canal. (Note that Line 4.2 does the same route clockwise.)

LINE 12
From Fondamente Nuove, this line calls at a number of Venice's outlying islands, including Murano, Torcello and Burano.

LINE N
This night service runs 11.30pm–4.30am daily from San Marco and San Zaccaria to the Lido via the Giudecca Canal and the Grand Canal. It is a cheap and spectacular way to see the city sights lit up at night.

Waterbus

Vaporettos are slow, single-storey waterbuses that chug along the major canals. They are flat-decked and fully accessible for wheelchairs, prams and buggies. Faster, more streamlined *motoscafi* travel to outlying islands, as do the large double-decker *motonavi* ferries. Waterbus stops are shown on most Venice maps and are clearly signposted around the city. All the departure quays *(pontile)* have route maps and timetables.

Tickets are available from ACTV booths, from machines at larger stops and also at some newsstands and tobacconists. Validate your ticket at the white electronic ticket reader near the entrance to the platform prior to boarding. Green ticket readers are "read only" and will not validate your ticket. If you are caught travelling without a validated ticket, you may be fined.

Traghetto

These are large unadorned gondolas which cross the canal at seven points between San Marco and the railway station from early morning until around 7 or 8pm (although they are not all always in operation). They have no fixed timetable; simply wait on a *traghetto* pier for the boat to arrive. Pay cash (€2 per person) to the oarsman as you board or leave the gondola. It is customary to stand up for the crossing, but you can opt to sit if you prefer. (Note that these vessels are not suitable for wheelchair users. Instead, use vaporetto Line 1.)

Gondola

Venice's traditional wooden gondolas are expensive and are used almost exclusively by tourists. There are several gondola ranks along the Grand Canal, including beside the Palazzo Ducale and Rialto, and also at busy pedestrian crossings along secondary canals. Official tariffs should be available at the dock. Expect to pay around €80 for the first 40 minutes, then €40 for additional 20-minute increments. After 7pm, prices are hiked. Before boarding, agree a price with the gondolier to avoid being overcharged.

Water Taxi

Small, sleek motorboats comprise Venice's water taxi fleet – an elite form of transport, which is reflected in the price. Expect to pay around €50–70 for a short hop within the city; and between €105 and €135 to travel from the airport to a city centre abode. Water taxis can hold up to ten people, making it a viable option if you are splitting the fare with family or friends.

Bus

In Venice, buses serve the mainland and the Lido only. The main bus station in Venice is at Piazzale Roma near the main train station. On the Lido, route A serves the north of the island, while route B heads south.

City buses in the Veneto are cheap and regular. Tickets, which must be bought prior to travel, are available from newsstands, tobacconists and shops that display the relevant bus company logo in the window. Tickets must be validated upon boarding.

People Mover

This high-tech elevated People Mover tramway shuttles passengers cheaply and rapidly between the city's three main arrival points: Marittima cruise terminal, the Tronchetto parking island and Piazzale Roma. It runs 7am to 11pm Monday to Saturday and 8am to 10pm (9pm in winter) on Sundays. It costs €1.50. Tickets are available at all three stations. You must scan your ticket to validate before travelling.

Walking

Venice is a tiny city and all the main sights in the *centro storico* are accessible on foot within half-an-hour of each other. It is also a city where getting lost in the tangle of alleyways *(calli)* is part of the attraction. Just remember to follow the frequent yellow signs on the walls indicating the direction of the main sights, keep to the right and keep moving on bridges.

Cycling

Cycling is not allowed in the city centre, but bike hire is popular on the mainland and on some of the islands in the lagoon, including the Lido. The **RideMovi** city bicycle scheme has a number of stations for bike hire in Marghera and Mestre, and three on the Lido.

RideMovi
W ridemovi.com

Driving

You can reach Venice by driving across the causeway but parking options are limited to garages. There is also a car ferry that commutes from the Tronchetto to the Lido.

Car Rental

There are a number of car rental offices at the airports and at Piazzale Roma for those wishing to explore the Veneto.

To rent a car you must be over 21 and have held a valid driver's licence for at least a year. Driving licences issued by any of the EU member states are valid throughout the EU. If visiting from outside the EU, you may need to apply for an International Driving Permit.

Rules of the Road

Drive on the right, use the left lane only for passing, and yield to traffic from the right. Seat belts are required for all passengers, and heavy fines are levied for using a mobile phone while driving. A strict drink-drive limit *(p146)* is enforced. During the day dipped headlights are compulsory when you are driving on motorways, dual carriageways and on all out-of-town roads. A red warning triangle, spare tyre and fluorescent vests must be carried for use in an emergency.

In the event of an accident or break-down, call the ACI emergency number (116) or the emergency services.

PRACTICAL INFORMATION

A little local know-how goes a long way in Venice. On these pages you can find all the essential advice and information you will need to make the most of your trip to this city.

AT A GLANCE

CURRENCY
Euro (EUR)

AVERAGE DAILY SPEND

SAVE €50	SPEND €100	SPLURGE €200+

COFFEE €1.50	Beer €5.00	DINNER FOR TWO €60

ESSENTIAL PHRASES

Hello	Buon giorno
Thank you	Grazie
Please	Per favore
Goodbye	Arrivederci/Ciao
Do you speak English?	Parla inglese?
I don't understand...	Non capisco

ELECTRICITY SUPPLY
Power sockets are type F and L, fitting two and three-pronged plugs. Standard voltage is 220-230v.

Passports and Visas

For entry requirements, including visas, consult the nearest Italian embassy or check the **ENIT** website. All visitors to Italy need a valid passport. Citizens of the UK, US, Canada, Australia and New Zealand do not need a visa for stays of up to three months but in future must apply in advance for the European Travel Information and Authorization System (**ETIAS**); roll-out has continually been postponed so check website for details. Visitors from other countries may also require an ETIAS, so check before travelling. EU nationals do not need a visa or an ETIAS.

ENIT
W italia.it
ETIAS
W travel-europe.europa.eu/etias_en

Government Advice

It is important to consult both your and the Italian government's advice before travelling. The UK Foreign, Commonwealth and Development Office (**FCDO**), the **US Department of State**, the **Australian Department of Foreign Affairs and Trade** and the Italian **Ministero della Salute** offer the latest information on security, health and local regulations.

Australian Department of Foreign Affairs and Trade
W smartraveller.gov.au
Ministero della Salute
W salute.gov.it
UK FCDO
W gov.uk/foreign-travel-advice
US Department of State
W travel.state.gov

Customs Information

You can find information on the laws relating to goods and currency taken in or out of Italy on the ENIT website.

Insurance

We recommend that you take out a comprehensive insurance policy covering theft, loss of belongings, medical care, cancellations and delays, and read the small print carefully.

UK and EU citizens are eligible for free emergency medical care in Italy provided they have a valid European Health Insurance Card (EHIC) or UK Global Health Insurance Card (**GHIC**). Australia has a reciprocal health care agreement with Italy and citizens can access essential medical treatment as long as they are registered to **Medicare**.

GHIC

W services.nhsbsa.nhs.uk/cra/start

Medicare

W servicesaustralia.gov.au

Vaccinations

No inoculations are needed to visit Italy

Money

Most places accept major credit, debit and prepaid currency cards. Contactless payments are becoming increasingly common in Venice, but it's always a good idea to carry some cash for small items and for *traghetti* fares. Cash machines (*bancomat*) can be found throughout the city.

Wait staff should be tipped €1–2 and hotel porters and housekeeping will expect €1 per bag or day.

Travellers with Specific Requirements

Venice has made a real effort to improve access for travellers with specific requirements, with 70 per cent of the centre now accessible to those with impaired mobility and most sites reachable by public transport. However, many older buildings may not have wheelchair access or lifts.

Most city museums are accessible and some offer induction loops and audio guides for the hearing impaired and partially sighted. Many bridges are fitted with low steps but no stair lifts, while all vaporetto stops are accessible for people with impaired mobility. The main routes 1 and 2 can carry up to four wheelchairs

and a discounted disabled ticket costs €1.50 including a carer.

Beyond Venice, all buses of the Mestre urban network and some of the Lido buses have extendable platforms and a designated area within them for wheelchairs.

The Venezia Accessibile information pack on the **Sanitrans** website lists barrier-free itineraries, accessible public toilets and travel arrangements, including manageable bridges. It also lists shops where you can hire wheelchairs. The **Comune di Venezia** website also includes itineraries designed for travellers with disabilities, as well as a map of accessible Venice, and the **Sage Travel** website is a great resource for more indepth information.

Comune di Venezia

W comune.venezia.it

Sage Travel

W sagetraveling.com

Sanitrans

W sanitrans.net

Language

Italian is the official language, though many people speak a Venetian dialect. English is widely spoken.

Opening Hours

Many museums are open daily. However, the times are subject to change, so it is wise to check ahead.

The main churches are usually open 10am–5pm Monday to Saturday.

On Mondays, some restaurants and attractions are closed.

Many shops close early on Sundays or for the day day.

Most shops, restaurants, museums and attractions close on public holidays.

Situations can change quickly and unexpectedly. Always check before visiting attractions and hospitality venues for up-to-date opening hours and booking requirements.

Personal Security

Venice is one of the safest cities in Europe. Serious crime is rare. Nevertheless, it is wise to take a few simple precautions. The historic centre is well policed, but pickpocketing is common. Leave important documents and valuables in a safe place and only carry the money you need. Be extra vigilant at train stations, markets, on public transport and at the landing stages of the vaporetti. After dark, stick to main thoroughfares rather than gloomy alleyways.

If you have anything stolen, report the crime as soon as possible at the nearest police station and take ID with you. Get a copy of the crime report (*denuncia*) to claim on your insurance. Contact your embassy or consulate if your passport is lost or stolen, or in the event of a serious crime or accident.

As a rule, citizens of Venice are very accepting of all people, regardless of their race, gender or sexuality. Homosexuality was legalized in 1887 and in 1982, Italy became the third country to recognize the right to legally change your gender. Due to a rise in anti-immigrant sentiment, some people of colour may experience racism.

AT A GLANCE

EMERGENCY NUMBERS

GENERAL EMERGENCY	AMBULANCE
113	**118**

FIRE SERVICE	POLICE
115	**112**

TIME ZONE
CET/CEST
Central European
Summer Time (CEST)
runs Mar–Oct.

TAP WATER
Tap water in Venice
is safe to drink -
water fountains are
dotted throughout
the city.

WEBSITES AND APPS

Venezia Unica
Tourist information for Venice
(*veneziaunica.it*).
Veneto Inside
Tourist information across the Veneto
(*venetoinside.com*).
CheBateo
Waterbus route and schedule app.
iBacari
App listing popular bars in the vicinity.
Hi!Tide Venice
Tide times and heights, to plan your route if the city floods.

Health

Italy has a world-class healthcare system. Emergency medical care in Italy is free for all UK, EU and Australian citizens (*p145*). If you have an EHIC or GHIC, be sure to present this as soon as possible. You may have to pay after treatment and reclaim the money later.

For other visitors, the payment of medical expenses is the patient's responsibility. It is therefore important to arrange comprehensive medical insurance prior to your visit.

Seek medical supplies and advice for minor ailments from pharmacies (*farmacie*). You can find details of the nearest 24-hour service on all pharmacy doors.

Smoking, Alcohol and Drugs

Smoking and vaping are banned in enclosed public places and the possession of illegal drugs is prohibited and could result in a prison sentence.

Italy has a strict limit of 0.5 g/l BAC (blood alcohol content) for drivers. This means that you cannot drink more than a small beer or a small glass of wine if you plan to drive. For drivers with less than three years' driving experience the limit is 0.

ID
By law you must carry identification at all times in Italy. A photocopy of your passport photo page (and visa if applicable) should suffice.

Responsible Travel
In response to the high volume of tourists visiting Venice, the #Enjoy-RespectVenezia campaign was launched in 2017 to raise awareness of tourist impact and to encourage responsible tourism in the city. The campaign asks that visitors follow certain rules to lessen their impact: walk on the right, do not linger on busy bridges, do not cycle in the city or lead bikes by hand. The steps of churches, bridges, wells, monuments and canalbanks are not picnic areas, nor are squares or *campi*.

Do not jump into the canals or attempt to swim in the lagoon, except at designated spots. Do not wear inappropriate clothing such as swimwear in the city. Don't drop litter or feed pigeons, and respect the privacy of local residents. Camping is also prohibited in the city, as is attaching padlocks to buildings or bridges, or buying fake goods from illegal street vendors.

From 2025, a new €5 tax on day trippers – the **Venice Access Fee** – is due to be implemented to help manage visitor numbers from the mainland and provide funds for maintenance and waste management. The tax will apply to all visitors over the age of 14. .

#EnjoyRespectVenezia
w comune.venezia.it
Venice Access Fee
w cda.ve.it/en

Mobile Phones and Wi-Fi
Wi-Fi is widely available throughout Venice, and cafés and restaurants will usually give you the password for their Wi-Fi on the condition that you make a purchase. Much of the city has wireless hotspots.

Visitors travelling to Italy with EU tariffs are able to use their devices abroad without being affected by roaming charges. Users will be charged the same rates for data, SMS and voice calls as they would pay at home. Visitors from other countries, with unlocked mobile phones, can buy an Italian pay-as-you-go SIM card.

Post
Stamps *(francobolli)* can be bought at post offices and *tabacchi*, which are recognizable by the black-and-white "T" sign.

Taxes and Refunds
VAT (called IVA in Italy) is usually 22 per cent, with a reduced rate of 4–10 per cent on some items. Non-EU citizens can claim an IVA rebate.

Discount Cards
The Venice tourist office, **Venezia Unica**, offers a range of discount cards to make visiting Venice easier on the purse strings. The silver, gold or platinum City Pass, which includes discounted museum, gallery and church entry, is available from €31.90 for children and seniors and €52.90 for adults. For young people aged 16–29 years, the €6 Rolling Venice pass and ACTV 3 Day Youth Pass provide a worthwhile travel discount (€22 for a three-day travel pass instead of €40) plus reduced entry to a number of sights.

ACTV also offers a variety of discounted travel cards *(biglietti a tempo)*, valid on all ACTV water and land routes for 24 hours (€25), 48 hours (€35), 72 hours (€45) or seven days (€65). They can be purchased at ACTV ticket booths, tobacconists *(tabacchi)* or online. All discount passes can be purchased online from Venezia Unica.
Venezia Unica
w veneziaunica.it

PLACES TO STAY

The city's island geography requires careful planning. Santa Croce, San Polo and Dorsoduro offer the greatest choice in the thick of things, while Castello, Cannaregio and Giudecca are good for quiet, period charm, and the Lido for beachy vibes. Easy access to a vaporetto stop is key.

Prices sky-rocket during the Carnival, Easter and the Film Festival, and are at their lowest from November to January. A tourist tax of €1–5 per night is applied to all overnight stays.

PRICE CATEGORIES

For a standard double room per night (with breakfast if included), taxes and extra charges.

....

€ under €150
€€ €150–350
€€€ over €350

San Marco

B&B Al Teatro

N5 **San Marco 2554** **bedandbreakfastalteatro.com · €**

You can't go wrong with booking a room at Eleonora's friendly B&B. It's located in her family's 15th-century palazzo and faces Teatro La Fenice, plus you'll have a lovely view of gondolieri gliding beneath your window. As a bonus, you can expect excellent local tips over a home-made breakfast.

Hotel Flora

P5 **San Marco 2283/A** **hotelflora.it · €€**

Fancy staying in a true San Marco gem? Run by generations of the Romanelli family, this heritage hotel is situated in an ivy-clad palazzo, tucked down a narrow street. Needless to say it oozes character; Rooms are decorated with antiques and offer views of their verdant pocket-sized garden, where breakfast and aperitivo is also served.

Hotel Rosa Salva

Q4 **Calle Fiubera 951** **rosasalvahotel.it · €€**

The name Rosa Salva is famous throughout Venice, thanks to the family's heritage pastry shop (conveniently, one can be found next door). This small hotel matches the high quality of their baking, with parquet flooring, sound-proofed windows and luxuriously big beds. There's an endless supply of excellent pastries for breakfast, too.

Corte di Gabriela

N4 **Calle Dei Avvocati 3836** **cortedigabriela.com · €€€**

If you're looking for something a little different, look no further than this chic design hotel in a period palazzo. Here, inventive styles combine frescoed rooms with contemporary design pieces. A (lavish) breakfast is served in the beautiful wisteria-draped courtyard, whose tables are an original plane of a Giudecca carpenter.

The Gritti Palace

N6 **Campo Santa Maria Del Giglio 2467** **marriott.com · €€€**

Guests won't need to leave the property to sightsee. Dating to 1525, this is Venice's most iconic heritage hotel, housed in the Doge's Palace on the Grand Canal. You'll feel like royalty among Rubelli's rich silk velvet wallpaper, heirloom antiques and rare marble-clad bathrooms – all as eye-watering as its prices, but totally worth it.

San Polo and Santa Croce

Al Ponte Mocenigo

D2 **Santa Croce 1985** **alpontemocenigo.com · €–€€**

A classic old-school Venetian hotel with all the period charm – think exposed beams, gilded beds, terrazzo floors – without feeling too over the top. That's thanks to friendly owners Sandro and Walter who hand out tips and recommendations over breakfast or drinks at the aperitivo bar.

Oltre il Giardino

📍 L2 🏠 San Polo 2542
🌐 oltreilgiardino-venezia.
com · €€

This unusual 1920s property, with its large sunny garden hidden behind a high wall, feels more like a country villa. Located near the Frari church, rooms feature paintings and portraits from the family's personal collection and restored furniture, giving each room a funky personality.

Hotel L'Orologio Venice

📍 N2 🏠 Riva de l'Ogio 1777
🌐 hotelorologiovenezia.
com · €€

While the rooms are modern and minimalist in design at this small chain hotel, each one has artworks created from the mechanisms of watches – the hotel's founder has a slight penchant for clock-making, you see. It's only a stone's throw from the Rialto market, too.

Aman Venice

📍 N3 🏠 San Polo 1364
🌐 aman.com · €€€

Quite simply the most beautiful hotel in Venice, the Aman is one of the most significant palaces on the Grand Canal: there's historically important art, Tiepolo frescoes and two gardens to take in. Its suites are the epitome of under-stated luxury, and you can treat yourself at its impeccable Italian restaurant and Aman spa.

Dorsoduro

La Calcina

📍 D5 🏠 Fondamenta Zattere Ai Gesuati 780
🌐 lacalcina.com · €–€€

Art critic and writer, John Ruskin, wrote *The Stones of Venice* in this small hotel in 1877. Now run by Marc and Regina, it remains as charming as ever with vintage Venetian décor and homely rooms offering fantastic views over the Giudecca Canal. Over summer, their in-house restaurant moves out to a pontoon on the water – bliss.

Palazzo Stern

📍 L5 🏠 3 Sestiere Dorsoduro 2792/A
🌐 palazzostern.com · €€

Gothic on the outside, Belle Epoque on the inside, and one of Venice's finest rooftop terraces: could this hotel get any better? The answer is yes; despite its prime Grand Canal position it's great value for money, plus they have a vintage wooden boat used for complimentary tours to Murano.

Hotel Avani Rio Novo Venice

📍 J4 🏠 Calle Larga Ragusei
🌐 lazzoexperimental.com
· €€–€€€

Book into Avani's bustling Rio Novo hotel, which is located near the university in a striking 1950s Rationalist building. Floor-to-ceiling windows in sleek contemporary rooms (including wheelchair-accessible options) overlook the waterways and scenic Venetian architecture. Tuck into classic *cichetti* at their ground-floor restaurant.

Il Palazzo Experimental

📍 B5 🏠 Calle Larga Ragusei 3489 🌐 nh-hotels.com · €€

The fun and fashionable come to play in the former headquarters of the Adriatica shipping company. Il Palazzo Experimental is the brainchild of Parisian mixology maestros the Experimental Group; it revolves around a top-notch bar and an excellent restaurant, with hyper-stylish interiors. You'll enjoy one of the best views of the city from the roof terrace, too.

Hotel Nani Mocenigo Palace

📍 C5 🏠 Fondamenta Nani 960 🌐 hotelnani mocenigo.com · €€€

Live like a Doge in this splendid 15th-century Venetian palazzo – it once belonged to Agostino Barbarigo, who commissioned many of the fine buildings on Piazza San Marco. The salons on the noble (principal) first floor feature frescoes and Murano chandeliers. The hotel also offers experiences, from creating your own Carnival mask to a private boat tour along the Grand Canal.

Cannaregio

Combo Venice

E2 🄰 Campo dei Gesuiti 4878 🅦 thisiscombo.com · €

For those who think hostels are just for backpackers, think again. This converted 12th-century monastery has a smart Scandi style, with shared and twin rooms, studios and apartments. Common areas include a laundry room, kitchen, bar-restaurant and luggage storage space, and regular art and music events provide plenty of opportunities to mingle.

Al Ponte Antico

P3 🄰 Calle Aseo 5768 🅦 alponteantico.com · €€€

Located in a quiet area of Venice's historic centre, this family hotel has its very own landing dock – perfect for water taxis dropping you off door-to-door. What truly makes it a cut above the rest, though, is its romantic terrace overlooking the Rialto Bridge.

Palazzo Abadessa

D2 🄰 Campiello Priuli 4011 🅦 badessa.com · €€–€€€

Evenings are magical in the hidden walled garden of this aristocratic 16th-century palace. Superior rooms have frescoes and canal views, while classic rooms are kitted out with plump beds fit for royalty. There's also an aperitivo hour and water taxis for visits to the opera.

Castello

Hotel Bucintoro

G4 🄰 Riva S Biasio 2135 🅦 hotelbucintoro.com · €

This warm wood-panelled hotel with views over St Mark's Basin makes you feel like you're afloat in a ship on the lagoon. While all rooms face the lagoon, the corner suite is the best with double aspect views. In warm weather, make the most of breakfast and aperitivo, both served alfresco on the sunny canalbank.

Residenza de L'Osmarin

F4 🄰 Calle Rota 4960 🅦 residenzadelosmarin.com · €€

Less than 300 metres from Piazza San Marco and only a few minutes' walk to the Gallerie dell'Accademia, Peggy Guggenheim Collection and Teatro La Fenice, you couldn't ask for a better location than Residenza de L'Osmarin. It's great for those seeking privacy or those looking to do their own thing; this lovely B&B is set on a quiet canal and offers mini-apartments with small kitchenettes.

Hotel Londra Palace

K7 🄰 Riva degli Schiavoni 4171 🅦 londrapalace.com · €€€

This smart hotel has been welcoming well-to-do guests in great style since 1853, including composer Tchaikovsky.

The interiors have a golden 19th-century sheen and the bar and restaurant are well frequented by Venetians, thanks to the excellent chef and roster of interesting cultural events held here.

The Northern Lagoon

Casa Burano

H1 🄰 San Martino Sinistro 506, Burano 🅦 casaburano.it · €

Step into the colourful postcard of Burano with a stay here. During the day, Burano is crowded with day-trippers, but at night it returns to the authentic fishers, island it is. Experience what it's like to live like a local Buranese with a stay in one of five quaint pastel-coloured cottages. To top it off, breakfast baskets are delivered daily. Yum!

Locanda Cipriani, Torcello

E6 🄰 Piazza Santa Fosca 29, Torcello 🅦 locandacipriani.com · €€

The country retreat of Giuseppe Cipriani (founder of glamorous Harry's Bar) and movie-star favourite, Hotel Cipriani provides a five-star service at affordable prices. Located on Torcello, it's also home to one of the best restaurants in the lagoon and is a great place to try Venetian classics like fried baby lagoon shrimps (*schie*).

Venissa Wine Resort, Mazzorbo Island

☉ H1 🏠 Fondamenta di Santa Caterina 3 🌐 venissa.it · €€€

Gourmet getaways are made in the shade of Venissa's revitalized vineyards. They produce Dorona grapes once favoured by the Doge, which you can sample at the Michelin-starred restaurant overlooking the vines. Then retire to one of five minimally-chic rooms furnished with high-end designer pieces set beneath ancient wooden beams.

The Southern Lagoon and Venice Lido

Villa Ines, Lido

☉ H2 🏠 Via Lazzaro Mocenigo 10, Lido 🌐 villa-ines.com · €

Owned by the famous Seguso glassmaking family, it goes without saying that the rooms at this Liberty-style villa are hung with extraordinary Murano chandeliers. The accolades don't stop there, as owner Marika runs the on-site Acquolino Cooking School, too.

JW Marriott Venice, Isole della Rose

☉ N4 🏠 Isola Delle Rose, Venice Lagoon 🌐 marriott.com · €€€

The Marriott is a private-island retreat located 20 minutes from San Marco (there's a free boat shuttle to ferry you back and forth). Most guests, however, find it hard to leave the fabulous facilities which include two restaurants, cooking school and family pool. The resort also has 12 fully accessible rooms.

Hotel Excelsior, Lido

☉ H2 🏠 Lungomare Marconi 41, Lido 🌐 hotel excelsiorvenezia.com · €€€

With its huge seaview terrace and private beach, this is the ultimate hotel in the Lido area. Its candy-coloured rooms are packed with movie stars during the Venice Film Festival, but you can experience the A-lister life with a private shuttle, which gets you to San Marco in 15 minutes.

Belmond Hotel Cipriani, Giudecca

☉ E6 🏠 Giudecca 10 🌐 belmond.com · €€€

When movie stars come to Venice, they stay at the Cipriani, due to the privacy afforded by its huge garden. There's the Olympic-sized swimming pool (the only one in Venice), Michelin-starred restaurant overlooking the lagoon and plush rooms and suites all with lagoon or garden views.

Padua, Vicenza and Verona

Portico Rosso, Vicenza

🏠 Contrà San Rocco 28, Vicenza 🌐 porticorosso.it · €

Set in Vicenza's historic district, the house of this B&B is nearly 600 years old – it used to belong to Count Valmarana, the uncle of the owner. Each room has its own name and this personable effect radiates through-out; the two owners go above and beyond to welcome you. During the summer, breakfast is served in the pretty, flower-filled garden.

Palazzo Mantua Benavides, Padua

🏠 Piazza Eremitani 18, Padua 🌐 palazzoman tuabenavides.com · €–€€

Once the home of scholar and professor Marco Mantua Benavides, this 16th-century mansion has been restored, with suites in the main house and apartments in the former stable. Needless to say there's an abun-dance of period character, and the heritage beauty theme continues at the UNESCO-listed Scrovegni Chapel, which is just a short walk away.

Due Torri, Verona

🏠 Piazza Sant'anastasia 4, Verona 🌐 hotelduetorri. duetorrihotels.com · €€€

Dive into the heart of Verona and around with a stay at Due Torri. Housed in a 14th-century palace in the heart of the historic district, the interior is as precious as you might imagine – but stay for the wealth of experiences they can organize for you. There's wine-tasting and panoramic bike tours, gelato and pasta cooking classes, and day trips to Venice all to choose from.

INDEX

PHRASE BOOK

In an Emergency

Help!	Aiuto!	eye-yoo-toh
Stop!	Fermati!	fair-mah-teh
Call a doctor.	Chiama un medico	kee-ah-mah oon meh-dee-koh
Call an ambulance.	Chiama un' ambulanza	kee-ah-mah oon am-boo-lan-tsa
Call the police.	Chiama la polizia	kee-ah-mah lah pol-ee-tsee-ah
Call the fire brigade.	Chiama i pompieri	kee-ah-mah ee pom-pee-air-ee

Communication Essentials

Yes/No	Si/No	see/noh
Please	Per favore	pair fah-vor-eh
Thank you	Grazie	grah-tsee-eh
Excuse me	Mi scusi	mee skoo-zee
Hello	Buon giorno	bwon jor-noh
Goodbye	Arrivederci	ah-ree-veh-dair-chee
Good evening	Buona sera	bwon-ah sair-ah
What?	Quale?	kwah-leh?
When?	Quando?	kwan-doh?
Why?	Perché?	pair-keh?
Where?	Dove?	doh-veh?

Useful Phrases

How are you?	Come sta?	koh-meh stah?
Very well, thank you.	Molto bene, grazie.	moll-toh beh-neh grah-tsee-eh
Pleased to meet you.	Piacere di conoscerla.	pee-ah-chair-eh dee-coh-noh-shair-lah
That's fine.	Va bene.	va beh-neh
Where is/are …?	Dov'è/ Dove sono …?	dov-eh/doveh soh-noh …?
How do I get to …?	Come faccio per arrivare a …?	koh-meh fah choh pair arri-var-eh ah …?
Do you speak English?	Parla inglese?	par-lah een-gleh-zh?
I don't understand.	Non capisco.	non ka-pee-skoh
I'm sorry.	Mi dispiace.	mee dee-spee-ah-cheh

Shopping

How much does this cost?	Quant'è, per favore?	kwan-teh pair fah-vor-eh?
I would like …	Vorrei …	vor-ray
Do you have …?	Avete …?	ah-veh-teh …?
Do you take credit cards?	Accettate carte di credito?	ah-chet-tah-teh kar-teh dee creh-dee-toh?
What time do you open/ close?	A che ora apre/ chiude?	ah keh or-ah ah-preh/ kee-oo-deh?
this one	questo	kweh-stoh
that one	quello	kwell-oh
expensive	caro	kar-oh
cheap	a buon prezzo	ah bwon pret-soh
size, clothes	la taglia	lah tah-lee-ah
size, shoes	il numero	eel noo-mair-oh
white	bianco	bee-ang-koh
black	nero	neh-roh
red	rosso	ross-oh
yellow	giallo	jal-loh
green	verde	vair-deh
blue	blu	bloo

Types of Shop

bakery	il forno /il panificio	eel forn-oh /eel pan-ee-fee-choh
bank	la banca	lah bang-kah
bookshop	la libreria	lah lee-breh-ree-ah
cake shop	la pasticceria	lah pas-tee-chair-ee-ah
chemist	la farmacia	lah far-mah-chee-ah
delicatessen	la salumeria	lah sah-loo-meh-ree-ah
department store	il grande magazzino	eel gran-deh mag-gad-zee-noh
grocery	la drogheria	lah droh-geh-ree-ah
hairdresser	il parrucchiere	eel par-oo-kee-air-eh
ice cream parlour	la gelateria	lah jel-lah-tair-ree-ah
market	il mercato	eel mair-kah-toh
newsstand	l'edicola	leh-dee-koh-lah
post office	l'ufficio postale	loo-fee-choh pos-tah-leh
supermarket	il supermercato	eel su-pair-mair-kah-toh
tobacconist	il tabaccaio	eel tah-bak-eye-oh
travel agency	l'agenzia di viaggi	lah-jen-tsee-ah dee vee-ad-jee

Sightseeing

art gallery	la pinacoteca	lah peena-koh-teh-kah
bus stop	la fermata dell'autobus	lah fair-mah-tah dell ow-toh-booss
church	la chiesa/ la basilica	lah kee-eh-zah lah ah-seel-i-kah
closed for holidays	chiuso per le ferie	kee-oo-zoh pair leh fair-ee-eh
garden	il giardino	eel jar-dee-no
museum	il museo	eel moo-zeh-oh
railway station	la stazione	lah stah-tsee-oh-neh
tourist information	l'ufficio di turismo	loo-fee-choh dee too-ree-smoh

Staying in a Hotel

Do you have any vacant rooms?	Avete camere libere?	ah-veh-teh kah-mair-eh lee bair-eh?
double room	una camera doppia	oona kah-mair-ah doh-pee-ah
with double bed	con letto matrimoniale	kon let-toh mah-tree-moh-nee-ah-leh
twin room	una camera con due letti	oona kah-mair ah kon doo-eh let-tee
single room	una camera singola	oona kah-mair-ah sing-goh-lah
room with a bath, shower	una camera con bagno, con doccia	oona kah-mair ah kon ban-yoh, kon dot-chah

I have a reservation.	Ho fatto una prenotazione.	oh fat-toh oona preh-noh-tah-tsee-oh-neh

Eating Out

Have you got a table for …?	Avete un tavolo per …?	ah-veh-teh oon tah-voh-loh pair …?
I'd like to reserve a table.	Vorrei prenotare un tavolo.	vor-ray preh-noh-tar-reh oona tah-voh-loh
breakfast	colazione	koh-lah-tsee-oh-neh
lunch	pranzo	pran-tsoh
dinner	cena	cheh-nah
the bill	il conto	eel kon-toh
waitress	cameriera	kah-mair-ee-air-ah
waiter	cameriere	kah-mair-ee-air-eh
fixed price menu	il menù a prezzo fisso	eel meh-noo ah pret-soh fee-soh
dish of the day	piatto del giorno	pee-ah-toh dell jor-no
starter	antipasto	an-tee-pass-toh
first course	il primo	eel pree-moh
main course	il secondo	eel seh-kon-doh
vegetables	i contorni	ee kon-tor-noh
dessert	il dolce	eel doll-cheh
cover charge	il coperto	eel koh-pair-toh
wine list	la lista dei vini	lah lee-stah day vee-nee
glass	il bicchiere	eel bee-kee-air-eh
bottle	la bottiglia	lah bot-teel-yah
knife	il coltello	eel kol-tell-oh
fork	la forchetta	lah for-ket-tah
spoon	il cucchiaio	eel koo-kee-eye-oh

Menu Decoder

l'acqua minerale	lah-kwah mee-nair- ah-leh	mineral water
gassata/ naturale	gah-zah-tah/ nah-too-rah-leh	fizzy/ still
agnello	ah-niell-oh	lamb
aglio	al-ee-oh	garlic
al forno	al for-noh	baked
alla griglia	ah-lah greel-yah	grilled
la birra	lah beer-rah	beer
la bistecca	lah bee-stek-kah	steak
il burro	eel boor-oh	butter
il caffè	eel kah-feh	coffee
la carne	la kar-neh	meat
carne di maiale	kar-neh dee mah-yah-leh	pork
la cipolla	la chip-oh-lah	onion
i fagioli	ee fah-joh-lee	beans
il formaggio	eel for-mad-joh	cheese
le fragole	leh frah-goh-leh	strawberries
il fritto misto	eel free-toh mees-toh	mixed fried fish
la frutta	la froot-tah	fruit
i frutti di mare	ee froo-tee dee mah-reh	seafood
i funghi	ee foon-ghee	mushrooms
i gamberi	ee gam-bair-ee	prawns
il gelato	eel jel-lah-toh	ice cream
l'insalata	leen-sah-lah-tah	salad
il latte	eel laht-teh	milk
il manzo	eel man-tsoh	beef
l'olio	loh-lee-oh	oil

il pane	eel pah-neh	bread
le patate	leh pah-tah-teh	potatoes
le patatine fritte	leh pah-tah-teen-eh free-teh	chips
il pepe	eel peh-peh	pepper
il pesce	eel pesh-eh	fish
il pollo	eel poll-oh	chicken
il pomodoro	eel poh-moh-dor-oh	tomato
il prosciutto cotto/crudo	eel pro-shoo-toh kot-toh/ kroo-doh	ham cooked/cured
il riso	eel ree-zoh	rice
il sale	eel sah-leh	salt
la salsiccia	lah sal-see-chah	sausage
succo d'arancia/ di limone	soo-koh dah-ran-chah/ dee lee-moh-neh	orange/lemon juice
il tè	eel teh	tea
la torta	lah tor-tah	cake/tart
l'uovo	loo-oh-voh	egg
vino bianco	vee-noh bee-ang-koh	white wine
vino rosso	vee-noh ross-oh	red wine
le vongole	leh von-goh-leh	clams
lo zucchero	loh zoo-kair-oh	sugar
la zuppa	lah tsoo-pah	soup

Numbers

1	uno	oo-noh
2	due	doo-eh
3	tre	treh
4	quattro	kwat-roh
5	cinque	ching-kweh
6	sei	say-ee
7	sette	set-teh
8	otto	ot-toh
9	nove	noh-veh
10	dieci	dee-eh-chee
11	undici	oon-dee-chee
12	dodici	doh-dee-chee
13	tredici	tray-dee-chee
14	quattordici	kwat-tor-dee-chee
15	quindici	kwin-dee-chee
16	sedici	say-dee-chee
17	diciassette	dee-chah-set-teh
18	diciotto	dee-chot-toh
19	diciannove	dee-chah-noh-veh
20	venti	ven-tee
30	trenta	tren-tah
40	quaranta	kwah-ran-tah
50	cinquanta	ching-kwan-tah
60	sessanta	sess-an-tah
70	settanta	set-tan-tah
80	ottanta	ot-tan-tah
90	novanta	noh-van-tah
100	cento	chen-toh
1,000	mille	mee-leh
2,000	duemila	doo-eh mee-lah
1,000,000	un milione	oon meel-yoh-neh

Time

one minute	un minuto	oon mee-noo-toh
one hour	un'ora	oon or-ah
a day	un giorno	oon jor-noh
Monday	lunedì	loo-neh-dee
Tuesday	martedì	mar-teh-dee
Wednesday	mercoledì	mair-koh-leh-dee
Thursday	giovedì	joh-veh-dee
Friday	venerdì	ven-air-dee
Saturday	sabato	sah-bah-toh
Sunday	domenica	doh-meh-nee-kah

ACKNOWLEDGMENTS

This edition updated by

Contributors Cristina Dainotto, Paula Hardy

Senior Editor Alison McGill

Senior Designers Laura O'Brien, Stuti Tiwari

Project Editor Aimee White

Editors Tavleen Kaur, Anuroop Sanwalia

Assistant Art Editor Divyanshi Shreyaskar

Proofreader Ruth Reisenberger

Indexer Kathryn O'Donoghue

Picture Research Manager Taiyaba Khatoon

Senior Picture Researcher Nishwan Rasool

Assistant Picture Research Administrator Manpreet Kaur

Publishing Assistant Simona Velikova

Jacket Designer Laura O'Brien

Jacket Picture Researcher Claire Guest

Cartography Simonetta Giori

Senior Cartographer James MacDonald

Senior DTP Designer Tanveer Zaidi

DTP Designers Rohit Rojal, Nityanand Kumar

Pre-production Manager Balwant Singh

Image Retouching-Production Manager Pankaj Sharma

Senior Production Controller Samantha Cross

Managing Editors Shikha Kulkarni, Beverly Smart, Hollie Teague

Managing Art Editor Gemma Doyle

Senior Managing Art Editor Priyanka Thakur

Art Director Maxine Pedliham

Publishing Director Georgina Dee

DK would like to thank the following for their contribution to the previous editions: Cristina Minoni, Charles Hebbert, Kate Hughes, Gillian Price.

The publisher would like to thank the following for their kind permission to reproduce their photographs:

Key: a-above; b-below/bottom; c-center; f-far; l-left; r-right; t-top

Alamy Stock Photo: Simona Abbondio 42br, Album 25t, Alessandro0770 25b, Alto Vintage Images 9cra, Antiqua Print Gallery 8–9b, Artefact 48b, Simone Padovani / Awakening 114, Bailey-Cooper Photography 37b, 65b, BasPhoto 80b, Piere Bonbon 34cra, Cinematic Collection 71t, Collection / Active Museum / Active Art 9br, Peter Delius 12crb, dpa picture alliance 99, Philip Dunn 12br, Greg Balfour Evans 13clb, Eye Ubiquitous / Mockford & Bonetti 134, eye35 123, Paolo De Faveri 92, Peter Forsberg 72, 78t, funkyfood London - Paul Williams 13cl, 24t, Gacro74 13bl, 132, Chicurel Arnaud / Hemis.fr 26, 40t, 88, 108b, © Fine Art Images / Heritage Images 28t, Hirarchivum Press 29cb, Historica Graphica Collection / Heritage Images 10tl, Peter Horree 60b, Image Professionals GmbH / LOOK-foto 104t, imageBROKER / Guenter Graefenhain 19, 36t, 52, 54b, imageBROKER / Ingo Schulz 76, imageBROKER / Lothar Steiner 68t, imageBROKER / Moritz Wolf 14, imageBROKER / Peter Fischer 129, Imageplotter 73b, INTERFOTO / Fine Arts 56, INTERFOTO / Personalities 57b, jessiemc / Stockimo 73t, Jon Arnold Images Ltd 115tl, Lebrecht Music & Arts / Music-Images 9tl, Library Archive 9crb, Melvyn Longhurst 35b, lowefoto 33t, Martin Thomas Photography 131t, Angus McComiskey 101t, Hercules Milas 20br, 38-39b, Sergey Novikov 113t, Giacomo Cosua / NurPhoto 11b, Panther Media GmbH / vvoennyy 71b, Chuck Pefley 37t, Andr Ph. 96b, Pictorial Press Ltd 10br, Prisma Archivo 10cla, Alex Ramsay 21bl, Really Easy Star / Giuseppe Masci 135, Really Easy Star / Toni Spagone 70, REDA &CO srl 47t, REDA &CO srl / Eddy Buttarelli 74b, Juergen Ritterbach 27t, 32t, robertharding / Carlo Moruccchio 69t, Felipe Rodriguez 107t, Matthias Scholz 117, Thierry GRUN - Aero 119, TRAVELSCAPES 33b, 67t, 128, Steve Tulley 30b, Viennaslide 47cr, Westend61 GmbH 11t, Scott Wilson 126, Wiskerke 83, Licht Wolke 35t, World History Archive 60t.

AWL Images: Jon Arnold 139, ClickAlps 54t.

Bevilacqua Tessuti: 91b.

Signor Blum: 104b.

Bridgeman Images: Cameraphoto Arte Venezia 29b.

Dreamstime.com: Adisa 120, Kuznetsov Andrey 41b, Baloncici 111, Brasilnut 110, Marco Brivio 133tl, Cristi Croitoru 42cb, 78b, 116, Dimabl 77, Dinogeromella 59b, Inna Felker 53, Ginger236 75t, Diana Gradeva 121tl, Laszlo Konya 15t, Engin Korkmaz 46–47b, Marktucan 42clb, Alberto Masnovo 81, 89tl, Zdenk Maty 43, Maudanros 15crb, Minnystock 5, 21tl, Martin Molcan 44, Yury Morozov 36b, 79, Mrreporter 57t, NatashaBreen 45b, Onlyfabrizio 42bl, Photogolfer 20cl, 40bl, Gianluca Piccin 67b, Oleksandr Ryzhkov 13clb (8),

Scaliger 16ca, Jozef Sedmak 108t, Smallredgirl 17, Stevanzz 21cr, Claudio Stocco 22t, 137, Tea 136, Christophe Testi 102b, ViliamM 95t, Vitalyedush 16cra, Vividaphoto 15cb, Yury 15clb.

© **Fondazione La Biennale di Venezia - ASAC:** Francesco Galli 12cr, Jacopo Salvi 10bl.

Fondazione Musei Civici di Venezia: Museo Correr 32b, 63t, Museo del Vetro, Murano 62h, Museo Storico Navale 63b.

Fondazione Teatro La Fenice: 87t.

Getty Images: De Agostini / DEA / F. FERRUZZI 39cr, De Agostini / DEA / G. DAGLI ORTI 58, Icas94 / De Agostini / DEA 8cla, Hulton Archive / Picture Post / Kurt Hutton / Stringer 59t, Moment Open / Filippo Maria Bianchi 41t, The Image Bank Unreleased / Sylvain Sonnet 27b, David Lees / Corbis / VCG 38cra.

Getty Images / iStock: E+ / JaCZhou 30–31t, E+ / tunart 6–7, Gargolas 85, minemero 13tl, Lesia Popovych 96t, RudyBalasko 12cra, underworld111 51.

L'Isola - Carlo Moretti: 90.

La Caravella: 93.

Palazzo Grassi S.p.A: Thomas Mayer 102t.

Peggy Guggenheim Collection: 49b, Matteo De Fina 48–49t.

Ristorante Linea d'Ombre: 105.

Shutterstock.com: 365 Focus Photography 74t, 4kclips 69b, Francesco Bonino 45t, ChiccoDodiFC 13cla, Doin 82, hlphoto 75b, marcus493 34b, Stefano Politi Markovina 23t, Andrei Molchan 31cra, nightcap 23b, Robert Harding Virleo 80t, Borls Stroujko 64–65t, Christian Vinces 28b, Walencienne 16crb.

Tragicomica: 98.

Venetia Studium: 91t.

Sheet Map Cover Image:
Getty Images / iStock: E+ / Alxpin.

Cover Images:
Front and Spine: **Getty Images / iStock:** E+ / Alxpin. *Back:* **Alamy Stock Photo:** funkyfood London - Paul Williams cl, Chicurel Arnaud / Hemis.fr tr, imageBROKER / Guenter Graefenhain tl.

All other images © Dorling Kindersley Limited
For further information see: www.dkimages.com

Illustrator: Chris Orr & Associates

First edition created by Book Creation Services Ltd, London.

A NOTE FROM DK

The rate at which the world is changing is constantly keeping the DK travel team on our toes. While we've worked hard to ensure that this edition of Venice is accurate and up-to-date, we know that opening hours alter, standards shift, prices fluctuate, places close and new ones pop up in their stead. So, if you notice we've got something wrong or left something out, we want to hear about it. Please get in touch at travelguides@dk.com

First edition 2002

Published in Great Britain by Dorling Kindersley Limited,
DK, One Embassy Gardens, 8 Viaduct Gardens,
London SW11 7BW, UK

The authorised representative in the EEA is
Dorling Kindersley Verlag GmbH. Arnulfstr.
124, 80636 Munich, Germany

Published in the United States by DK Publishing,
1745 Broadway, 20th Floor, New York, NY 10019, USA

A CIP catalog record for this book
is available from the British Library.

A catalog record for this book is available
from the Library of Congress.

ISSN: 1479-344X
ISBN: 978-0-2416-7686-8

Printed and bound in China

www.dk.com